THE SUPERVISORY ALLIANCE

THE SUPERVISORY ALLIANCE
Facilitating the Psychotherapist's Learning Experience

Edited by SUSAN GILL

JASON ARONSON INC.
Northvale, New Jersey
London

This book was set in 11 pt. New Baskerville by Alpha Graphics of Pittsfield, NH, and printed and bound by Book-mart Press, Inc. of North Bergen, NJ.

Library of Congress Cataloging-in-Publication Data

The supervisory alliance : facilitating the psychotherapist's learning experience / [edited] by Susan Gill
    p. cm.
   Includes bibliographical references and index.
   ISBN 0-7657-0307-6
   1. Psychoanalysis—Study and teaching—Supervision. 2. Psychodynamic psychotherapy—Study and teaching—Supervision. 3. Psychotherapists—Supervision
  of. I. Gill, Susan.

  RC502.S86 2001
  616.89'17'071—dc21

                           00-046440

Printed in the United States of America on acid-free paper. For information and catalog write to Jason Aronson Inc., 230 Livingston Street, Northvale, NJ 07647-1726, or visit our website: www.aronson.com

Contents

PART II—WORKING WITH COUNTERTRANSFERENCE

Acknowledgments

I want to express my gratitude to my husband, Peter Unger, whose emotional and intellectual support has sustained me for the better part of a lifetime. I thank him particularly for his help with my work on this book.

I also want to thank the Postgraduate Center for Mental Health, where I first trained as a social work intern. Working in Postgraduate Center's Adult Clinic, I was impressed by the training staff; they all combined a sharp intelligence with an acute sensitivity to the needs of their clients. This prompted me to continue as an analytic candidate at Postgraduate Center's Psychoanalytic Institute, and then to participate in its training program in Supervision of the Psychoanalytic Process. This program, directed by Stanley Teitelbaum, has stimulated many of the papers in this book.

To my supervisors and supervisees, I give thanks for all you have taught me.

Contributors

Sydney W. Arkowitz, Ph.D., is on the faculty of the Southwest Center for Psychoanalytic Studies, where she serves as vice president of the board, and where she teaches, supervises, and does training analyses. She is past president of the Southwest Psychoanalytic Society and Director of Training of the Psychology Internship Program at the University of Health Sciences Center, Department of Psychiatry, University of Arizona. She is the winner of the Menninger Award, granted by the American Psychoanalytic Association, for her paper "The Overstimulated State of Dyslexia: Perception, Knowledge, and Learning."

Anne E. Bernstein, M.D., F.A.P.A., is a Clinical Professor of Psychiatry at the Columbia University College of Physicians and Surgeons. She is an Attending Psychiatrist at the New York Presbyterian Hospital, Collaborating Psychiatrist at New York State Psychiatric Institute, and Collaborating Psychoanalyst at the Columbia University Psychoanalytic Center for Training and Research. She has appointments in Liaison and Forensic Psychiatry at the Columbia University Medical Center. The author of numerous books and papers, in 1991 she received the first Nancy C. Roeske Award for outstanding and continuing contributions to medical education from the American Psychiatric Association.

William J. Coburn, Ph.D., is a faculty member and past board member of the Institute of Contemporary Psychoanalysis in Los Angeles and clinical instructor at Cedars Sinai Medical Center, Department of Psychiatry, Los Angeles. Dr. Coburn is past Program Chair of Division 39 of the Southern California Chapter of the American Psychological Association. The recipient of the 1999 Daphne S. Stolorow Memorial Essay Award, he has published and presented articles on countertransference, subjectivity, supervision, and other related areas.

Mary Beth M. Cresci, Ph.D., is Dean of Training of the Psychoanalytic Institute of the Postgraduate Center for Mental Health. She is a faculty member, Senior Supervisor, and Training Analyst in the Adult Psychoanalytic Program and a faculty member in the Training Program in the Supervision of the Psychoanalytic Process.

Lawrence Epstein, Ph.D., is a Fellow, Training, and Supervising Analyst at the William Alanson White Institute; and a Clinical Professor of Psychology in the Postdoctoral Program in Psychotherapy and Psychoanalysis, Adelphi University.

Susan Gill, Ph.D., C.S.W., is a Supervisor and faculty member in the Adult Training Program of the Psychoanalytic Institute of the Postgraduate Center for Mental Health, and the Psychoanalytic Psychotherapy Study Center, and is a Supervisor at the Washington Square Institute for Psychotherapy and Mental Health. Dr. Gill has published and presented clinical papers on working with resistance, transference, projective identification, and sexual abuse. Her papers have appeared in the *International Forum of Psychoanalysis*, *Psychoanalytic Social Work*, and *The Clinician*. In 1997, she received Postgraduate Center's Emanuel K. Schwartz Memorial Award for writing on psychoanalytic supervision. Before becoming a psychoanalyst, Dr. Gill received a Ph.D. in art history and taught at Parsons School of Design and Hunter College. She was a frequent contributor to art journals, and she co-authored the book *Théophile-Alexandre Steinlen*. She maintains a private practice in New York City.

Howard E. Gorman, M.D., Ph.D., F.R.C.P.C., is a faculty member in the Department of Psychiatry at the University of Toronto, and is a Psychiatrist and Psychotherapy Supervisor at the Centre for Addiction and Mental Health in Toronto. Prior to entering medical training he received his Ph.D. in mathematics from the University of Chicago and subsequently taught mathematics at Roosevelt University in Chicago and at Stanford University in Palo Alto, California. He has published journal articles on the role of interpretation in supervision, and on expanding the definition of the psychoanalytic attitude.

Winslow Hunt, M.D., has for the past fifteen years been in the private practice of psychiatry and psychoanalysis in Pocatello, Idaho. During much of this time he has been an examiner for the American Board of Psychiatry and Neurology. He now teaches in the Family Practice Residency Program at Idaho State University. Prior to moving to Pocatello he practiced in New York City where he was Associate Professor of Clinical Psychiatry at the College of Physicians and Surgeons, Columbia University. Dr. Hunt received his undergraduate training at the University of Chicago and his medical and psychiatric training at Columbia University. A graduate of the New York Psychoanalytic Institute, he is the author of a number of articles in psychiatric and psychoanalytic journals, principally in the area of countertransference.

Susan C. Katz, M.D., graduated *magna cum laude* from Barnard College and received her medical training at Columbia College of Physicians and Surgeons, completing a psychiatry residency at New York State Psychiatric Institute. She is currently engaged in private psychiatric practice in Tucson, Arizona, where she lives with her husband of twenty-seven years and three sons. She is a member of the American Society of Clinical Psychopharmacology.

Iris Levy, C.S.W., is a faculty member, Senior Supervisor, and Training Analyst in the Adult Training Program, the Psychoanalytic Institute, Postgraduate Center for Mental Health. Formerly affiliated with Bellevue Psychiatric Hospital, she received her M.S.W. from New York University. In 1993, she was the recipient of the Postgraduate Center's Emanuel K. Schwartz Memorial Award for the chapter in this volume, and in 2000 she was the recipient of the Postgraduate Center's Arlene and Lewis Wolberg Memorial Award for her paper on the "Laius Complex."

Wilma Cohen Lewis, Ph. D., is a faculty member, Senior Supervisor, and Training Analyst in the Adult Psychoanalytic Training Program, the Psychoanalytic Institute, Postgraduate Center for Mental Health, where she also serves as a faculty member in the Training Program in the Supervision of the Psychoanalytic Process. She is a faculty member and Supervisor at the Training Institute for Mental Health and an Adjunct Assistant Professor of Psychology and Education, Department of Clinical Psychology, Teachers College, Columbia University.

Carol Martino, C.S.W., is a Supervisor in the Adult Training Program at the Psychoanalytic Institute, Postgraduate Center for Mental Health. She is a member of the Postgraduate Center Psychoanalytic Society, as well as the Association for Psychoanalytic Self Psychology. The recipient of the Emanuel K. Schwartz Memorial Award, presented by the Postgraduate Center for Mental Health for writing on psychoanalytic supervision, in 2000, she has a full-time private practice in New York City.

Susan Reifer, C.S.W., is a psychoanalyst and family and couples therapist in private practice in New York City. She is an Adjunct Assistant Professor at Columbia University School of Social Work and has taught at the Wurzweiler School of Social Work, Yeshiva University. She is a Supervisor in the Adult Training Program, the Psychoanalytic Institute, Postgraduate Center for Mental Health, where she was formerly the coordinator of the Continuing Education Program.

Jennifer Lyons Roberts, C.S.W., is a Supervisor and faculty member in the Adult Training Program at the Psychoanalytic Institute, Postgraduate Center for Mental Health, New York City. As a former coordinator for the Institute for Performing and Creative Artists at the Postgraduate Center, Ms. Lyons Roberts specializes in working with performing and creative artists in her private practice in New York City.

Stanley H. Teitelbaum, Ph.D., is Director of the Training Program in Supervision of the Psychoanalytic Process at the Postgraduate Center for Mental Health in New York City, where he also serves as a Training Analyst, Senior Supervisor, and faculty member. He is Dean of Training at the Contemporary Center for Advanced Psychoanalytic Studies in Teaneck and Livingston, New Jersey. Dr. Teitelbaum, who is widely published in professional journals, is best known for his writing in the field of psychoanalytic supervision and for his book *Illusion and Disillusionment: Core Issues in Psychotherapy.*

Introduction

SUSAN GILL

Contemporary developments in the field of psychodynamic supervision have shifted from an authoritarian model, with a didactic approach, to a relational model, in which the interpersonal dynamics between the supervisor and supervisee are seen as central to the development of a productive learning experience. It is now recognized that promoting effective supervision depends, to a great extent, on a positive supervisory alliance and there is a greater awareness today that, for many, the supervisory process can produce anxiety and promote feelings of vulnerability (Jaffe 2000). Consequently, supervisors are becoming more sensitive to narcissistic issues of vulnerability and anxiety, inherent in the supervisory process, that affect their trainees. The chapters in this volume offer a framework for understanding these issues and discuss methodologies for dealing with them.

Part I, "Facilitating the Psychotherapist's Learning Experience," offers an introduction to psychodynamic supervision and a variety of insights into working with anxiety and vulnerability.

Stanley H. Teitelbaum outlines some of the contemporary developments in psychoanalytic theory and practice that have had a significant impact. Such developments include the emergence of the relational model mentioned above, an increasing awareness of how the supervisory relationship is internalized, and the impact of developmental theory, with its emphasis on the holding environment and attention to empathic ruptures. In addition, Teitelbaum points out the importance of supervisors recognizing their own blind spots and negative internalizations, or "supertransferences" (Teitelbaum 1990).

Susan Gill talks about the vulnerability inherent in being a supervisee in terms of ego ideals and self-exposure. She highlights the dual nature of mastery involved in being, at once, the knowing therapist and the unknowing supervisee. Supervisees compare their ideal self with their experienced self (Schafer 1967), and this can lead to feelings of failure and humiliation. While the supervisory experience is intended to produce professional growth, it can generate feelings of frustration and shame. To address these feelings, specific interventions are suggested.

Sydney W. Arkowitz examines many aspects in the supervisory relationship that create vulnerability. Perfectionism, for example, often serves to mask underlying anxieties that need to be examined in order that they be mastered by the supervisee. This perfectionism can lead to self-denigration and self-mortification for the learner who, naturally, cannot meet such exacting standards. Among the many useful ideas for dealing with the supervisee's anxieties, Arkowitz proposes that the supervisor act as a model of a softened ego ideal, one who recognizes the elusive nature of perfection. Arkowitz also discusses the value of the supervisor modeling how she arrives at psychodynamic formulations: allowing the supervisee to see the constant shifts that occur in the supervisor's thinking, as assessment and understanding unfold. This helps the supervisee to see that such formulations are not arrived at magically.

Susan Reifer describes three models to help with supervisory anxiety: patient-centered, therapist-centered, and process-centered, and she discusses the value of making a learning diagnosis of defensive coping styles in order to choose the most empathic approach for each individual.

Wilma Cohen Lewis gives a moving personal account of her own anxiety as a supervisee and offers an effective approach to easing such anxiety, taken from her own work as a supervisor. She emphasizes the need to dilute the transference, thus limiting negative superego projections from the supervisee to the supervisor.

Jennifer Lyons Roberts also recounts her own experience as a supervisee. She uses the concept of stage fright, which she sees as a universal phenomenon, to highlight feelings such as shame, guilt, and separation anxiety that are stirred up in the act of performing, whether on stage or in front of an audience of one—the supervisor.

Iris Levy points out that candidates often feel more anxious in supervision than they do in analysis. While the analyst is expected to be relatively neutral and nonjudgmental, in supervision evaluation is a part of the process. Fear of being judged creates a fertile ground for the development of punitive superego projections. Through her case example, Levy shows that such projections can be modified by respecting the student's individual style of learning, and by developing a positive supervisory alliance using "supervisory neutrality."

Carol Martino uses a self psychology approach to supervision, showing how supervisees experience selfobject transferences that coincide with the developmental phases of the learning process. She maintains that if the supervisees' selfobject needs are met, a more open ambience emerges, creating a greater dialogue between the supervisory pair. Martino uses Wolf's (1995) concept of the "disruption–restoration sequence" as it applies to "restoring the bond between teacher and student when an empathic failure has occurred." Using detailed clinical examples, she shows the efficacy of this model in her ability to stay closely attuned to subtle shifts in the supervisee's responses to the supervisor's interventions.

An interesting phenomenon emerges from these chapters, written from a variety of theoretical perspectives: the goal of the supervisor is to create a safe space where she can establish a genuine and spontaneous relationship with the supervisee. And, in order to achieve this goal, it is essential that the supervisor be closely attuned to the subjectivity, or emotional experience, of the supervisee within the supervisory relationship. While many of the authors look at this idea through a classical lens, they arrive at solutions similar to those advanced by contemporary relationists, interpersonalists, and intersubjectivists (see Berman 2000).

The value of an interpersonal model is confirmed by Mary Beth M. Cresci, who writes about a study she made at an analytic training institute to see what created an optimal responsiveness to learning in supervision. She discovered that it was not the theoretical orientation of the supervisor that was paramount, but the manner and personality of the supervisor: The supervisor who made the supervisee least anxious was perceived by the supervisee to be the better teacher.

Part II, "Working with Countertransference," is devoted to a controversial subject. Should the supervisor encourage the disclosure of countertransference by the supervisee? The chapters make the case that, if handled sensitively and judiciously, working with countertransference can be a valuable part of the supervisory process.

Lawrence Epstein's chapter provides a transition from the first to the second part of the book. In exploring how the supervisor can create an optimal learning environment, he exposes his own mistakes with a supervisee and shows that by failing to take into account the supervisee's self-esteem, he created a supervisory impasse. Epstein describes how this error helped him to develop a more effective means of working with his supervisees. In addition, he offers cases in which he addresses his supervisees' countertransferences to their patients. He shows how he works to normalize and validate the widest possible range of feelings for the supervisee. Through his vivid examples, Epstein demonstrates that when supervisees are able to value the feelings aroused by their patients, they can begin to explore their meaning.

Winslow Hunt, in several clinical vignettes, describes the positive use of countertransference in his work with psychiatric residents. He believes that countertransference often illuminates core components of the therapeutic relationship. Hunt emphasizes the maintenance of boundaries so that the supervisor can work toward the supervisee's understanding her countertransference feelings, without overly intruding into her personal life.

Howard E. Gorman uses a lively clinical example that demonstrates how he effectively interpreted a supervisee's countertransference and shows how this led to the understanding of a collusion between the patient and the therapist. Gorman describes how this understanding created greater collegiality between the therapist and the supervisor, as well as opening up a stalemated treatment between the therapist and his patient.

Anne E. Bernstein and Susan C. Katz describe a most unusual situation in which both the supervisor and the supervisee had dreams about the patient that shed light on the case. Through process material from both the therapeutic and supervisory dyads, they show that a strong supervisory alliance can lead to an exchange of rich unconscious material between the learner and the teacher.

William J. Coburn describes a situation in which the supervisor disclosed her own feelings of countertransference during a supervisory session. This disclosure shed light on the feelings of both the supervisee and his patient. Coburn describes how hearing the supervisor's disclosure helped the supervisee to feel understood on a deeply emotional level. Thus the supervisor modeled empathic attunement that could be internalized by the supervisee and created the potential for a developmental experience. Coburn describes these phenomena from an intersubjective perspective.

REFERENCES

Berman, E. (2000). Psychoanalytic supervision: the intersubjective development. *International Journal of Psychoanalysis* 81:273–290.

Jaffe, L. (2000). Supervision as an intersubjective process: hearing from candidates and supervisors. *Journal of the American Psychoanalytic Association* 48:561–570.

Schafer, R. (1967). Ideals, the ego ideal, and the ideal self. *Psychological Issues* 5:131–174.

Teitelbaum, S. (1990). Supertransference: the role of the supervisor's blind spots. *Psychoanalytic Psychology* 7:243–258.

Wolf, E. (1995). How to supervise without doing harm: comments on psychoanalytic supervision. *Psychoanalytic Inquiry* 15: 252–267.

I

Facilitating the Psychotherapist's Learning Experience

The Changing Scene in Supervision

STANLEY H. TEITELBAUM

Scholarly attention to the various dimensions of psychoanalytic supervision appears to be catching up with the interest in
many of the current issues within psychoanalysis itself. The advent
of new developments within psychoanalysis in recent years has had
a considerable impact on the scope and purview of psychoanalytic
supervision. The number of training programs within psychoanalytic institutes is currently growing, each program imparting to
supervisors-in-training an ever-widening body of knowledge and
principles of supervision.

Whereas in the early days of psychoanalytic training it was
thought that the most experienced analysts and faculty would be
the best supervisors, it is now recognized that a separate set of acquired skills is necessary in order to become a capable supervisor
of the psychoanalytic process.

Supervision has historically been viewed as a situation in which
one person, considered to be more or less of an expert (i.e., pos-
sessing super vision), helped another analyst to deepen her under-

standing of case material. In this model supervision was primarily didactic, and patient oriented; that is, the patient's psychodynamics and defenses and the analyst's understanding of psychoanalytic theory and technique were the core foci of the supervisory experience. In other words, the teaching–learning focus chiefly revolved around the enlightenment of the supervisee by the supervisor with regard to such issues as how to listen with the third ear, how to establish and maintain a working relationship, how to distinguish latent from manifest content, and how to work with dreams, resistance, and transference.

One of the early and prolonged controversies among supervisors took shape around the question of whether the appropriate realm of supervision was didactic or experiential. For those who promoted the didactic approach the rationale was that there was a body of psychoanalytic knowledge to be taught and learned, and that the supervisees' personal reactions, countertransferences, and feelings about the supervision itself were not a primary focus.

For those who espoused the idea that supervision is best conducted with an experiential focus, the rationale was that in order for supervisees to be of most help to their patients, it was of paramount importance for them to more fully and deeply understand the countertransference nature of their reactions to their patients and the obstacles (problems about learning) that interfere with productive analytic treatment. Although this issue was often dichotomized and passionately argued among psychoanalytic supervisors at regular supervisors' meetings at established training institutes, in many ways it became a straw man. Ultimately, most supervisors acknowledge their adherence, in differing combinations, to both points of view. In effect, both theoretical and technical content as well as countertransference impediments were deemed the relevant spheres to be addressed in ongoing supervision.

As a result of increased awareness of the realm of psychoanalysis as a two-person psychology, many theorists maintain that the role of the analyst is not that of a detached observer and interpreter of what goes on within the patient, but rather that of a participant in the psychoanalytic process and an integral part of the very process she is attempting to observe and understand. The relational model, with its emphasis on how participants in the therapeutic relationship impact upon one another in a variety of ways, which in turn influence the course of treatment, has a carryover effect to the field of psychoanalytic supervision.

In the early literature on supervision, the prevailing view was that a highly knowledgeable and problem-free supervisor pointed out and pursued the learning problems and countertransference obstacles within the supervisee. When there were conflicts and difficulties in the supervision, it was assumed that these were a function of the unresolved problems within the supervisee. The blind spots and interferences in the teaching–learning dimension that emanated from the supervisor were seldom considered. I (Teitelbaum 1990) have referred to this process as supertransference. In the current supervisory climate it is frequently recognized that both supervisee and supervisor may be contributing to supervisory difficulties, misattunements, and stalemates. Accordingly, supervisors of today are more often open to acknowledging their part in supervisory conflict and impasses, as well as to exploring their part in the ripple effect of the parallel process in which issues from the supervisory interaction may be played out in the treatment arena.

THE SUPERVISORY RELATIONSHIP AS A CORE DIMENSION IN PSYCHOANALYTIC SUPERVISION

Although attention to the phenomenon of parallel process (Doehrman 1976, Searles 1955) and its development as a core concept in psychoanalytic supervision created a shift in emphasis to the study of the importance of what takes place in the supervisory relationship, it took many years before full recognition was given to the value of focusing on the supervisory relationship per se as a window into the treatment process between analyst and patient. In addition, a greater appreciation for the importance of creating a positive supervisory alliance in order to promote effective supervision has developed. In the past it was more or less taken for granted that students eagerly came to supervision to learn about their cases; it is now recognized that for many supervisees the establishment of a safe supervisory atmosphere is a necessary precondition for openness and learning to take place. There is a greater awareness today that for many analysts-in-training the supervisory process under certain circumstances can be more threatening, anxiety arousing, and promoting of feelings of vulnerability and danger than one's personal analysis. Hence, the supervisory relationship itself increasingly has come to be viewed as a central dimension of the supervisory process. As Rock (1993) has observed, "The theory of supervision has moved from a didactic to a relational model, with an emphasis on the mutuality of the process of influence. The influence of the supervisory relationship itself on what is learned, how it is learned, and what effect it has on the therapy being supervised is the central area of concern" (p. 4).

Along with a heightened sensitivity by supervisors to the students' reactions to the supervision, a democratization of the supervisory relationship has occurred. Just as a change in the balance of power between the patient as consumer and the analyst as provider has taken place, so, too, has psychoanalytic supervision relinquished its authoritarian model. With regard to the patient–therapist relationship, Modell (1991) has noted that "the egalitarian ideals of our society, combined with a critical consumerism, have effectively removed therapists from a position of authoritative infallibility from which they treat the patient's criticism as a transference distortion" (p. 19). In a similar vein, Gill (1979) has taken the position that it is increasingly recognized that certain idiosyncratic relations of patients to their therapists may actually be a function of real aspects of the therapist's personality. These observations are equally pertinent to the supervisory relationship.

Although supervisors continue to wield considerable power in the assessment of a candidate's readiness to move along within a training institute, this partial change in the balance of power has replaced a more extreme, earlier model in which supervision was essentially a "tilted relationship" (Greenacre 1959) in which one party (the supervisee) was relatively powerless, dependent, and deferent in relation to another person (the supervisor), who determined the supervisory agenda. Currently, there appears to be a tendency toward a greater degree of openness on the part of the supervisee with regard to her reactions to the supervision, along with a greater readiness to express dissatisfaction about areas of the supervision.

This development has provided an increased opportunity for supervisors to utilize their knowledge of parallel-process phenomena. For example, it is commonly observed that a patient who is invested in warding off defective feelings about herself will criticize the therapist for her flaws, deficiencies, and technical errors. In so doing the patient will often astutely press the very buttons about which the therapist is most sensitive. The therapist, defensive about these areas in which she feels inadequate or deficient, may ward this off by being critical of the supervisor for an approach that does not resonate with the therapist's. The supervisor, in turn, feels unjustly, inappropriately, or overly attacked and can use this experience as a barometer for what is going on in the treatment situation. This situation would be an example of parallel process as it plays out in an upward direction. The element of the therapist's ability to confront the flaws in the supervisor provides a more intense affective understanding of what may be going on between patient and therapist.

Supervisor sensitivity to the narcissistic issues in the training of analysts, together with a knowledge of parallel-process phenomena, has led to refinements in supervisory techniques for dealing with the technical errors presented by the analyst in supervision. For example, in describing his attempt to elicit more feelings from a patient immersed in isolation of affect, an analyst reported in supervision the following intervention: "I'm struck by the feeling that I had that there is some feeling in you in all of this [material], related to all of this, and somehow you have told me all these facts and still haven't gotten to it." The analyst was puzzled by the patient's ensuing silence. The supervisor recognized that this intervention was ineffective because it made the patient feel accused of not going about the treatment in the right way. Hence, instead of didactically demonstrating improved technique, which would have been experienced as critical by the supervisee, the supervisor framed his intervention in the form of an evocative question: "This patient is very sensitive to nuances and prone to feel criticized. Might you think of any alternative way to get him to look at this warding off of feelings?" In this way the supervisor was able to work on the analyst's technique while at the same time circumventing an upward parallel process in which the supervisor critically impacts on the analyst in a way similar to the analyst's impact upon the patient.

The increasing democratization of the supervisory relationship has also paved the way for supervisors to nondefensively explore their own blind spots, or "supertransferences" (Teitelbaum 1990). No longer are conflicts in supervision attributed solely to the unresolved problems and interferences in learning emanating from the supervisee. The anxieties, defenses, self-esteem issues, and the like of the supervisor are all now considered as legitimate contributions to misunderstandings, miscommunication, and misalliance in the supervisory relationship. (This point will be discussed more fully later in this chapter.)

Another aspect of the supervisory relationship that has received recent attention is the role of gender issues. Leighton (1994) has distinguished between masculine and feminine supervisory styles. The former is stereotypically characterized as having a focus on the understanding of theoretical constructs and a relative lack of attention to the supervisee's affective needs and is more patient-centered, while the latter is presumed to have a greater emphasis on the supervisory rapport and is a more therapist-centered model of supervision. I believe that we have already seen a shift toward a more nurturing style of supervision in which the supervisor is more sensitive to the needs and feelings of the supervisee. This shift has occurred as a result of theoretical advances which emphasize the importance of empathic connectedness. Applying Leighton's analysis, one might predict that this trend toward nurturing supervision is likely to accelerate as the field of psychoanalysis is increasingly populated by women. Further examination of supervisor–supervisee pairings in which the supervisor's style and the supervisee's preferred mode of learning are studied would be a productive area of research.

INTERNALIZATION OF THE SUPERVISOR

Considerable interest has developed in recent years in the ways in which the supervisory relationship is internalized. In thinking back over past supervisory experiences, most analysts vividly recall aspects of the supervisory atmosphere that were pivotal in the learning that took place, as well as in the development of their professional identity as psychoanalysts. To the extent that the supervisee experiences a superego component to the interventions of the supervisor, a critical versus a supportive supervisory attitude is often internalized by the supervisee, and this can have a major impact or effect on the learning attained. Thus, supervisees often internalize the way in which they felt treated by their supervisors. Some supervisees are able to learn from a critical supervisor who points out all the errors in the thinking, technique, and interpretations of the supervisee. More often, however, it is the validation offered by the supervisor that has a profound and lasting effect in the analyst's development. Positive internalizations are frequently revealed in such memories as "the most important thing was that he gave me validation for what I knew," "he was encouraging and supportive," "she was a model for how to be in the field."

In discussing the psychoanalytic process, Arlow and Brenner (1990) have pointed out that "in the course of analysis, bit by bit, piece by piece, the analysand introjects the calm, nonjudgmental, understanding analyst and reconstitutes him or her as a good object within the superego" (p. 683). A similar process of assimilation and internalization can be thought of as an inherent feature of psychoanalytic supervision. Just as there has developed a greater appreciation for the importance of the therapeutic action of psychoanalysis, so, too, a new emphasis is being given to the effect of the internalization of the supervisor and the supervisory atmosphere.

Increasing emphasis is being given to the need to cultivate the supervisory alliance as a precondition for meaningful teaching-learning to take place. While this may seem obvious to the trained supervisor of today, it is a dimension that was often erroneously taken for granted in the past. Supervisees need to develop a feeling of trust that the supervisory atmosphere is a benign one, that they can feel safe in exposing themselves in spite of the evaluative component of the supervision, and that the supervisor is earnestly interested in being there for the supervisee in a way that meets her learning needs and professional development. If this dimension is meaningfully attended to via a supportive, encouraging, and validating supervisory atmosphere, then a teaching–learning focus can evolve around issues in theory, technique, the listening process, countertransference, and so on.

Casement (1985) has described the importance of the "internalized supervisor," particularly in the early stages of psychoanalytic training, when the candidate is most in need of the comments and suggestions provided by the supervisor. He states,

> When a student therapist begins to work with training cases under supervision, the supervisor has a crucially important function in holding the student during this opening phase of clinical work—while he or she is learning to hold the patient analytically. The supervisor provides a form of control, making it safe for the therapist and patient to become analytically engaged, and helping a student to understand and to contain what is being presented by the patient. [p. 31]

Casement views this process of acquiring an "internalized supervisor" as a precursor to a later stage of professional identity in which the analyst, now capable of functioning in a more autonomous way, carries around her own "internal supervisor." Reliance on one's own well-grounded and individualistic way of doing the analytic work is the essence of the "internal supervisor." Hence, Casement envisions this as a developmental process in the growth of the analyst, in which "the shift from an initial dependence upon the external supervisor, via the internalized supervisor, to a more autonomous internal supervision is a slow process" (p. 46).

It is worth noting again that negative internalizations of the supervisor may also occur and can have a deleterious effect on the development of the supervisee. Among the more common scenarios that may lead to a negative internalization are (1) supervisors with their own agendas and needs who insensitively address and interpret neurotic dynamics or character problems in the supervisee, and (2) supervisors who have difficulty containing their competitiveness and ambitions and need to demonstrate their superior interpretations about the patient's psychodynamics. They may thereby undermine the supervisee's creativity and autonomy by too often offering their own insights and solutions and dismissing those of the supervisee.

A supervisory style that centers around the supervisor routinely telling the therapist "what to do" with her patients may often lead to the therapist feeling oppressed and hindered by the presence of the supervisor's injunctions when she is in the treatment room with patients. One student with this type of negative internalization reported on the freeing effect he experienced in his work with a patient when he was no longer discussing the patient in supervision. He said, "I realized the extent to which I had felt oppressed and restrained by the symbolic presence of the supervisor when I was in supervision with him. I needed to exorcise his impact in order for me to be more myself with my patients." It is important for supervisors to have an appreciation for the constraining influence that the therapist may experience from this type of supervision.

THE IMPACT OF SUPERVISION
UPON THE SUPERVISOR

With the advent of the discovery of the role of parallel process in supervision, we have become more sensitive to how the feelings and reactions of the supervisor are influenced by reenactments from the supervisee's work with her patients (as well as the converse, in which the analyst's work with patients involves a carrying out of interpersonal themes occurring in the supervisory relationship).

What we are coming to acknowledge to a greater degree is that not only the analyst, but also the supervisor, brings a set of needs to the supervisory relationship. The supervisor–supervisee relationship is made more complex by the legitimate narcissistic needs of the supervisor, such as the wish to mentor, that is, the need to feel she is making a meaningful contribution, along with more neurotic needs, such as disciple-hunting; competitiveness with the analyst-in-training, other supervisors, or the candidate's training analyst; the need to bolster or enhance her reputation at the institute through the supervisee; and so forth. It is of central importance to recognize the nature of these anxieties within the supervisor, and to understand the ways in which they impact upon what takes place in the course of the supervision.

Given these complexities it is understandable that there are many supervisory impasses; I believe that these impasses occur much more frequently than has been previously acknowledged. Another cause of supervisory failures and misalliances comes about as a result of the supervisor's difficulty in shifting gears, that is, in not modifying her teaching position vis-à-vis the analyst, as the latter's needs change during the course of the supervision.

In describing the importance of how the analyst meets the needs of the patient, Casement (1991) states, "A part of the consistency that a patient needs from the analyst is that of empathic responsiveness to changing needs, which means the analyst sometimes adapting to the patient rather than remaining rigidly the same. In this too, the analyst parallels early mothering" (p. 333). Similarly, supervisors are now more cognizant of and responsive to the need to adapt their supervisory approach to the point the supervisee has reached in her learning and development, in contrast to earlier times, when the prevailing position was that "this is the point of view that I have to offer, and I expect the supervisee to be receptive to my way of thinking and working." In other words, there is a greater readiness than heretofore on the part of the supervisor to adapt to the needs of the supervisee, rather than expecting that the supervisee will "fit in" with the approach of the supervisor.

I also believe that there is a growing atmosphere of openness in studying the causes of supervisory impasses, rather than simply defensively attributing the problems to the "difficult supervisee." It is a reflection of progress that supervisors of today are freer to acknowledge and explore their own contributions to supervisory misalliances than heretofore, when the prevailing view was that the supposedly well-analyzed supervisor did not bring his own unresolved issues to the supervisory setting.

Currently, we are able to study the supervisory relationship as both a meaningful source of data as well as a legitimate province of sensitivity. Supervisors and supervisees are often unaware of the ways in which they are impacting upon each other and may even misjudge their impact. It is not unusual for the supervisory participants to have divergent experiences of a supervisory session.

In one supervisory setting a relatively inexperienced supervisor felt a need to inform the supervisee how helpful she (the supervisor) might be because of her extensive knowledge of the type of patient being presented by the supervisee. The analyst felt unacknowledged for her abilities in understanding her patient and felt implicitly criticized by the supervisor. As the session continued the analyst became increasingly defensive in the presentation of her work. The supervisor, unaware that the analyst's defensiveness was related to something that she perceived in the supervisor's attitude toward her, attempted to make teaching points about the concept of projective identification. The analyst felt misunderstood and a misalliance followed.

In another example, an experienced supervisor made interventions designed to validate the analyst's skill in providing a holding environment for a fragile borderline patient. He felt that the supervisee was quite sensitive to the needs of the patient and was attempting to confirm this in his feedback to the supervisee. The analyst viewed herself to be lacking in basic theoretical and technical knowledge, so she experienced the supervisor's statements as a confirmation that she did not know the work. She came away from the session feeling criticized.

These examples speak to the importance of gauging our impact on our students and of determining the extent to which our experience of the supervision is in gear with theirs. In the examples cited the supervisees were readily forthcoming about their reactions to the supervisor's interventions, and the divergence in the experience was immediately apparent and could be metabolized. The greater danger occurs in those situations in which the supervisee does not feel free to openly share such reactions, and the supervisor, being unaware of them, proceeds on a wavelength that is discordant from the supervisee's. Since a supervisory misalliance or impasse may develop out of such experiences, it would seem that a worthwhile supervisory technique would be to periodically check out with the supervisee how she reacted to a particular approach or to a segment in the supervision. This type of occasional monitoring can serve to promote and safeguard the supervisory alliance. I believe that we are reaching a point in supervision in which the supervisor can feel less pressured about having to be omniscient and can even experience a greater degree of openness and readiness about learning new things from her supervisee.

IMPLICATIONS OF CURRENT PSYCHOANALYTIC THEORY FOR SUPERVISION

Theoretical advances in psychoanalytic treatment have a corresponding impact upon the way in which supervisory goals and expectations are perceived and considered. Many of the concepts from object relations theory, self psychology, and developmental ego psychology are now being utilized by psychoanalytic supervisors in the way in which they think about and approach the supervisory work. For example, themes in the current scope of psychoanalytic supervision include the following: supervision as a developmental process involving the phases of separation-individuation, the importance of the holding environment for the supervisee, awareness of the internalization of the supervisor and the supervisory attitude as a crucial dimension, attention to empathic ruptures emanating from the supervisor, and the prevalence of narcissistic issues for the supervisee.

The recent interest in the four psychologies described by Pine (1990) as drive, ego, object, and self may also impact on the way in which a supervisor approaches the supervision. Does a supervisor adhere to a singular theoretical orientation, or does the supervisor attempt to facilitate the therapist's understanding of the patient's material from different vantage points? Is there a correlation between the supervisor's theoretical predilections and the style of supervision? Are supervisors who follow a drive-theory framework more likely to conduct patient-centered supervision, while supervisors with a self psychology orientation more likely to be attuned to the self-esteem needs of the supervisee? These are some of the questions that await further investigation.

NONTHEORETICAL DEVELOPMENTS AFFECTING PSYCHOANALYTIC SUPERVISION

There are several additional nontheoretical developments occurring within psychoanalysis that have exerted an influence on the field of psychoanalytic supervision. I am referring here to such things as the changing balance of supply and demand between students and supervisors at many psychoanalytic training institutes, and the impact of managed care upon psychoanalytic treatment.

With regard to the former, as the roster of supervisors has increased and the enrollment of candidates has decreased at many institutes, supervisees have assumed a greater freedom and a more appropriate sense of entitlement vis-à-vis the supervisory relationship. Consequently, supervisees of today are more assertive than past supervisees in expressing their negative feelings when their supervisor is late, answers the phone during a session, changes appointment times, or announces a vacation with short notice. These disruptions would most likely have been overlooked on an overt level in the past, and through the process of identification and modeling the supervisee student might present herself in a similar way to patients. The expectation would be that such interferences would be nonissues and overlooked in a manner corresponding to the way the analyst responded to the supervisor. I propose that there are many things like these that are part and parcel of the supervisory attitude and supervisory atmosphere, and that affect the course of supervision and ultimately have impact on the treatment sessions of the supervisee.

With the advent of managed care and its increasing encroachment upon psychoanalytic treatment, the composition of our supervisees' caseloads has taken an increasing turn in the direction of psychotherapy and short-term therapy cases. As a result, the supervisory focus may increasingly shift away from issues like the understanding and analysis of transference and working through, and may require a greater emphasis on such dimensions as development of the working alliance, early resistances in treatment, ongoing management problems, and issues in early termination. It is becoming increasingly challenging for analysts and supervisors alike to develop ways in which they creatively pursue the application of psychoanalytic concepts and techniques to the shifting trends in caseloads. Arlow and Brenner (1988), in discussing the future of psychoanalysis, suggest, "We can therefore anticipate an accentuation of a trend which is already apparent, namely, changes in the formal elements of psychoanalytic technique—therapy two or three times a week, often without the couch, interruptions in therapy, etc." (p. 11). Friedman (1993) has cautioned that one of the painful truths of current psychoanalytic training is that we may be preparing candidates to work with cases which they may not have. In the environment of managed care it behooves supervisors to have more flexible expectations and attitudes concerning the analyst's needs in supervision. Hence, an emphasis on techniques in short-term therapy and the role of more active techniques utilizing psychoanalytic principles may become a legitimate aspect of ongoing psychoanalytic supervision.

As the nature of psychoanalytic practice changes, one might speculate about other modifications that might develop in the practice of psychoanalytic supervision. Will senior analysts who experience a decline in their own caseload attempt to fill open hours by devoting more time to doing supervision? Will the traditional format of once-a-week supervisory contact become modified if economic adversity impacts upon supervisees? Would reduced frequency be effective? Will supervisors move in the direction of offering group supervision as a way to safeguard their income? Will telephone supervision become a growing trend?

In summary, the emergence of the many new developments within psychoanalysis has necessarily had an impact on psychoanalytic supervision. It is anticipated that attention to these developments will continue to have an enriching impact on both supervisors and supervisees.

REFERENCES

Arlow, J., and Brenner, C. (1988). The future of psychoanalysis. *Psychoanalytic Quarterly* 57:1–14.
——. (1990). The psychoanalytic process. *Psychoanalytic Quarterly* 59:678–692.
Casement, P. J. (1985). *Learning from the Patient.* New York: Guilford.
——. (1991). The meeting of needs in psychoanalysis. *Psychoanalytic Inquiry* 11(3):325–345.

Doehrman, M. (1976). Parallel processes in supervision and psychotherapy. *Bulletin of the Menninger Clinic* 40:3–104.

Friedman, L. (1993). *The objective truth controversy: How does it affect tomorrow's analysts?* Paper presented at the Fourth Annual International Federation for Psychoanalytic Education Conference, New York, November.

Gill, M. (1979). The analysis of the transference. *Journal of the American Psychoanalytic Association* 27 (Suppl.):263–288.

Greenacre, P. (1959). Certain technical problems in the transference relationship. *Journal of the American Psychoanalytic Association* 7:488–502.

Leighton, J. (1994). *Are all supervisory styles created equal? Bifurcation and gender bias in didactic modes.* Paper presented at the Conference on Gender Issues in the Supervisory Relationship, Postgraduate Center for Mental Health, New York, March.

Modell, A. (1991). The therapeutic relationship as a paradoxical experience. *Psychoanalytic Dialogues* 1(1):19–28.

Pine, F. (1990). *Drive, Ego, Object, and Self.* New York: Basic Books.

Rock, M. (1993). *Effective supervision.* Paper presented at the Fourth Annual International Federation for Psychoanalytic Education Conference, New York, November.

Searles, H. (1955). The informational value of the supervisor's emotional experiences. In *Collected Papers on Schizophrenia and Related Subjects*, pp. 157–176. New York: International Universities Press.

Teitelbaum, S. H. (1990). Supertransference: the role of the supervisor's blind spots. *Psychoanalytic Psychology* 7:243–258.

2

Narcissistic Vulnerability in Supervisees: Ego Ideals, Self-Exposure, and Narcissistic Character Defenses[1]

SUSAN GILL

INTRODUCTION

The psychotherapy supervisee works toward the formation of a professional identity with a specific goal: the attainment of professional competence. Integral to being a supervisee are issues about knowledge and mastery that raise anxiety and questions of self-esteem in the trainee. How does the supervisee perceive he is performing with his client? How is his work viewed by his supervisor? How well will he progress toward his goal of being a psychotherapist? These issues permeate the supervisee's world and, particularly in the supervisory relationship, they create powerful feelings of narcissistic vulnerability. How the supervisee negotiates challenges to his sense of self, and what role the supervisor plays in this chal-

1. I would like to thank Dr. Wilma Cohen Lewis for several valuable discussions on the supervisory relationship.

lenge, profoundly affect the course of the supervisee's professional development.

In this chapter I will examine the influence of the ego ideal in shaping the internal experience of the supervisee, as well as other elements that affect his narcissistic equilibrium, such as self-exposure. I'll also explore more difficult self-esteem problems, as seen in a supervisee with narcissistic characterological defenses. Finally, some ideas about the supervisor's role in addressing these vulnerabilities will be discussed.

THE *EGO IDEAL* AND THE *IDEAL SELF*

Freud (1914) first used the term ego ideal in "On Narcissism: An Introduction":

> We have learnt that libidinal impulses undergo the vicissitude of pathogenic repression if they come into conflict with the subject's cultural and ethical ideas . . . Repression . . . proceeds from the ego; we might say with greater precision, that it proceeds from the *self respect* [italics added] of the ego . . . man has set up an *ideal* in himself by which he measures his actual ego . . . This ideal ego is now the target of the self-love which was enjoyed in childhood by the actual ego. The subject's narcissism makes its appearance displaced on to this new ideal ego, which like the infantile ego, finds itself possessed of every perfection that is of value . . . and when as he [man] grows up, he is disturbed by the admonitions of others and by the awakening of *his own critical judgement* [italics added], so that he can no longer retain that perfection, he seeks to recover it in the new form of an ego ideal. What he projects before him as his ideal is the substitute for the lost narcissism of his childhood in which he was his own ideal. [pp. 93–94]

According to Freud (1914) the ego ideal is a kind of substitute for the earliest days of existence, when the infant is his own omnipotent ideal, undifferentiated from the mother. At the moment that he realizes he is not one with his mother, he projects this omnipotence outward, creating the ego ideal. And, no matter how well he integrates that part of himself given over to this "ideal," he is always seeking to return to the original state of narcissistic equilibrium, when he was one with the object. The desire to return to this original state of omnipotence and narcissistic perfection provides the impetus that becomes "the *primum movens*" of education and activity in many other spheres of life (Chasseguet-Smirgel 1985). Within this context, the aspirations of the supervisee as represented in his ego ideal become a powerful motivator for his learning.

Before continuing, it will be helpful to clarify the terms *ego ideal* and the *ideal self*. The latter term was developed after Freud, and it seems particularly well-suited to the purposes of this chapter. Implicit in Freud's notion of the ego ideal discussed in the 1914 paper, quoted above, was a certain conception of the self—one that is referred to by the phrase "self-respect." Since Freud used the same term *das Ich* to refer both to the self and to the ego, there has been much confusion about these terms. (See Modell [1993], Morrison [1986], Sandler et al. [1963], Schafer [1967].) And, because Freud (1923) used the terms *ego ideal* and *super-ego* interchangeably after he introduced the structural theory in *The Ego and the Id*, there has also been confusion about the similarities and differences between those two concepts.

In the many attempts to unravel the meanings of the ego versus the self and the super-ego versus the ego ideal (see Sandler et al. 1963), a number of writers have redefined Freud's original term, the ego ideal, as the ideal self. One of these formulations is especially helpful here and that is Schafer's notion of the *ideal self* and the *experienced self*. The former is an image of oneself that satisfies a specific ideal and the latter is an image of oneself as one thinks one is. "Whenever one measures his performance against his own standards, he is comparing experienced and ideal self-representations" (Schafer 1967, p. 151).

Freud's concept of the ego ideal is relevant to supervision in that it helps to better define an integral part of the supervisee's experience. Throughout the course of learning, the supervisee is continually confronting himself and his image of himself: "Ego ideals inspire growth, learning, and the wish for mastery. The gap between one's ego ideals and the perception of one's actual self and actual performance tests self-esteem" (Jacobs et al. 1995, p. 212). To put this another way, problems and tensions that arise between the experienced self and the ideal self affect narcissistic strivings and can lead to feelings of failure and humiliation. Both in establishing the initial supervisory frame and in monitoring the supervisory alliance for narcissistic tensions that might arise, it is essential that the supervisor be aware of this vulnerability.

Another important factor affects the supervisee's narcissistic equilibrium: the dual nature of mastery involved in the task of learning to be a psychotherapist. As a therapist, the supervisee is required to perform as something of an authority—if he is not yet an expert, he must appear to know a good deal more than the patient who is seeking his help, displaying some degree of mastery. As a student, he is clearly less knowledgeable than his supervisor, and, in the supervisory relationship, he displays his mastery in a very different way. There he is, at once, the "knowing" therapist and the "unknowing" supervisee. This dual function compounds his vulnerability because he must shift back and forth between two opposing poles that correspond with two quite different self-representations. Opposing self-representations foster intrasystemic conflict, even as the supervisee strives to integrate the two ego ideals, "the self who knows" and the "self who seeks to learn."[2] The

---

2. Rangell describes two kinds of intrapsychic conflict: (1) intrapsychic conflict traditionally referred to in the literature that pertains to *intersystemic* phenomena as between the ego and the id and the ego and superego, for example, and (2) intrapsychic conflict as it pertains to *intrasystemic* conflict. This involves choice-dilemmas in which the ego or superego, for example, is in conflict with itself (Rangell 1969).

duality of roles, tasks, and self-representations creates an added level of vulnerability and, in a phrase from Ford (1963), it puts the supervisee in a "condition of double jeopardy."

NARCISSISTIC VULNERABILITY OF THE SUPERVISEE

The narcissistic vulnerability of the supervisee, particularly of the beginning trainee, has been noted in the literature on psychoanalytic supervision since the early 1960s. In his 1962 paper, "Problems of Psycho-Analytic Supervision," Searles states: "We need to see how vulnerable he [the supervisee] is to feeling caught between the patient's intense criticism on the one hand and the supervisor's disapproval on the other, so that his beleaguered areas of healthy self-esteem very much need our support and encouragement" (p. 587).

In a study of psychiatric residents as to choice of profession and acquisition of a therapeutic role and identity, Ford (1963) found that "conflict rises from the anxiety induced in doing psychotherapy. This is almost unique among professional pursuits in that the actual control mechanism of the psychiatrist's personality—his perceptual ego—is under constant probing and provocation from the anxious energy transferred by his patient . . . the student is in a condition of double jeopardy from the anxiety transferred by his patient and proceeding from his affective involvement with his supervisor" (p. 478).

In Fleming and Benedek's (1966) book on psychoanalytic supervision, Spitz is mentioned as having noted that supervision is experienced as more dangerous than analysis. Tischler (1968) talks about vulnerability in the supervisory relationship: "The beginning resident's exquisite sensitivity to the supervisor's receptivity makes the supervisor-supervisee relationship extremely vulnerable to interpersonal innuendo and leads to the censoring of process material and careful selection of cases for presentation. . . . In more extreme instances, the resident's sensitivity may be so extreme that the slightest criticism is interpreted as a rejection . . ." (p. 419).

In this article, students were interviewed about their supervisory experiences. One supervisee told the writer "screening what I report depends more upon who I feel safe with."

Brightman (1984) uses a Kohutian model to describe "the process of change in the area of professional narcissism" for the psychotherapy trainee. He describes four developmental stages of the psychotherapy learning process:

> (1) an initial defensive denial of data contradicting an image of the therapist-self as omniscient, benevolent, and omnipotent, to (2) identification with an idealized professional figure who supports and values the trainee even as such conflicting data enter the supervision, to (3) a loss and mourning of the grandiose professional self in the face of the evidence that undermines it, to (4) the establishment of a new, less perfectionistic ego-ideal, derived in part from the supervisory identification. [p. 312]

In her paper on perfectionism in the supervisee, Arkowitz (1990) discusses ways in which supervision can contribute to a "modification of the supervisee's ego ideal, softening of superego structures, and increasing relinquishment of grandiosity . . ." (p. 54).

It is clear that the supervisee must confront specific stressors that heighten his narcissistic vulnerability in the supervisory relationship.

SUPERVISION AND THE EGO IDEAL

Learning to be a psychotherapist differs from learning in many other professions because the thoughts and feelings, personality and behavior of the therapist play such a major role in how he conducts himself professionally.[3] In meeting with a supervisor on

---

3. Developments in relational and intersubjective theory in which the therapist's subjectivity is viewed as an integral part of the intersubjective field (patient–therapist relationship) highlight this fact. See Stolorow and colleagues (1994).

a regular basis, the supervisee inevitably feels that he is exposing himself not only in terms of his professional competence, but also in terms of his basic personality (thoughts and feelings, both conscious and unconscious).

Moreover, he is dependent on the supervisor to evaluate his performance and pass him on to the next phase of his training. By its very nature, this evaluative function has a regressive-inducing impact on the supervisee that contributes to his vulnerability: one that evokes memories, associations, and fantasies of his personal history as a student vis-à-vis his teachers and a child vis-à-vis his parents.

Because psychoanalytic supervision is conducted in a dyadic relationship, it contains unconscious parallels with many other important relationships for the supervisee: the parent and his child, the supervisee and his patient, the supervisee and his therapist, to name just three.[4]

Because of these parallels, unconscious object relationships evoked in supervision can heighten, or reawaken, archaic conflicts regarding the ego ideal: "Narcissistic balance and the capacity for self-regard are intertwined with self-representations. Coupled with self-loving and self-critical feelings are object-representations of loving and valuing or hostile and critical objects. The degree of integration the trainee has achieved over loving and hostile representations will influence his ability to withstand external criticism or antagonism from patients, colleagues, or supervisors while preserving some stability of self-esteem" (Jacobs et al. 1995, p. 213). So, while the supervisory experience, by nature of its emotionally charged complexity, can be a potential source of growth for the supervisee, it can also be a source of conflict, frustration, and shame.

---

4. Parallel process in regard to patient-supervisee and supervisee-supervisor has been a rich topic in the supervision literature. For a comprehensive bibliography on the topic see Rock (1997).

SELF-EXPOSURE

Self-exposure is an integral part of the supervisory process and a significant source of narcissistic vulnerability. The supervisee exposes his work, whether in the form of verbatim process notes or discussions of his work with his supervisor. The supervisee's clinical ability, basic intuition, intelligence, personal feelings, and blind spots are all exposed, making him highly vulnerable. Moreover, he is always holding himself up to ideals that he wishes to achieve. Sometimes these ideals propel him forward, but sometimes they hold him back.

For example, the ideal of the neutral, nonjudgmental therapist leads to the misconception, especially in beginning therapists, that they are not supposed to react emotionally to their patients. Here, I do not mean how they behave with their patients, but how they feel about their patients. Even when beginning therapists are taught about the productive use of countertransference, this remains in the realm of theory. Usually it takes the supervisee considerable time to develop the ability to talk about his emotional responses. This seems especially true in terms of negative or angry emotions. Consequently, supervisees may keep their feelings hidden, not only from their supervisors, but from themselves. In viewing beginners in a one-way mirror in the course of a supervisory training program, this was a ubiquitous phenomenon.

Case Vignette

A was presenting a case in which the client began to act out in the treatment. The patient was coming very late to her sessions, often with little more than ten minutes left. She would cancel appointments and the therapist would create make-up sessions that she would then miss. While we focused on the dynamics and transference issues that were contributing to this acting out, I would sometimes ask the supervisee how he felt

while waiting for the patient. For months, there was little response from him on this. Some eight or nine months after the
start of supervision, the supervisee went to the clinic specifically to see the patient, who did not come to her session. In
reviewing this material in supervision, the supervisee was able
to say that as he sat waiting and wondering where his patient
was he felt frustrated and angry. This disclosure on his part
was clearly a breakthrough for him and also for our work in
supervision. We were now able to use the therapist's feelings
(countertransference) to better understand the patient's dynamics. The supervisee's ability to accept and acknowledge his
negative feelings was clearly a result of his professional growth
and developing self-confidence.

Another student seemed to guard against exposing his concrete concerns about a client, fearing he would not seem analytically minded. Searles (1962) makes the point that the supervisee
is often reluctant to talk about his emotional responses because
he fears the supervisor will not think him "sufficiently analytic."

Case Vignette

B was working with a difficult patient with three small
children. The supervisee was aware that the patient induced
a great many countertransference reactions and wanted to
address specifically how to deal with boundary problems he
was having with the patient. We were able to make some head-
way on these problems. Toward the end of the semester, which
corresponded with the therapist terminating with this patient,
the supervisee expressed a great deal of anxiety around the
patient's behavior. The nature of this anxiety was diffuse and
unclear. We continued to focus on the supervisee's process
notes in which his patient told him about losing his temper
with his children. While there was no direct expression of

parental abuse, it appeared to me from the material the supervisee presented that he might be worried about the patient's potential physical abuse of his two small children. However, the supervisee was unable to verbalize this to me. His concern emerged when I reflected to him that he seemed worried about the patient's children. In discussing some of his difficulties in bringing this up with me, he spoke of his uncertainty about whether his concern was justified, as well as his concern about the appropriateness of these worries. He believed this was beyond the scope of his work with the patient and might be seen as nonanalytic. So there was anxiety and fear around this topic, one of these fears being that I might respond by telling the supervisee that this "should not" be his concern. The supervisee was much relieved when I took these concerns seriously and was able to discuss various ways in which he might handle them.

In the first vignette, the supervisee's ideal of being a benign, nurturing, and neutral therapist kept him from acknowledging feelings that he considered to be antithetical to this ideal. In the second, the supervisee's ideal of being analytically minded made it difficult for him to acknowledge extra-analytic concerns. In both examples, the supervisees' fear of exposure kept them from seeing and acknowledging feelings that went against their internal ideals. In each of these cases, the supervisee seemed to be experiencing a blind-spot that impeded the progress of the work.

Attunement to the affective state of the supervisee helped the first trainee to identify a hidden feeling, and it helped the second to clarify a problem that was creating anxiety. In each case, the supervision provided a holding environment (see Casement [1985], Rock [1997], and Winnicott [1960]) that allowed the supervisee safely to explore uncomfortable feelings, or blind spots, evoked by his patient. And, by helping the supervisee to acknowledge thoughts and feelings that seemed unacceptable, and even shameful, I was normalizing these thoughts and feelings. By saying, "What you are feeling is normal and natural. It's part of the job," I validated the supervisee's subjective experience and, in doing that, I helped bridge the gap between his ideal self and his experienced self.

THE NARCISSISTIC SUPERVISEE

In the discussion and vignettes above, I described narcissistic vulnerability as a regular component of the supervisee's learning experience. Now, I turn to narcissistic vulnerability that is more problematical, in students with narcissistic character defenses. In such supervisees, susceptibility to narcissistic wounds, and vulnerability to low self-esteem, is intensified, and this intensified vulnerability makes them defend in ways that create significant "problems about learning."[5] (On supervisory characterological issues see Arkowitz [1990], Brightman [1984], Glickauf-Hughes [1994], Mehlman [1974], and Sharaf and Levinson [1964].)

My experience with a supervisee who presented with a variety of narcissistic character defenses has helped me to recognize some of the components of this defensive constellation. I will describe three of these defenses.

1. In presenting his work to me, the supervisee often referred to his "special" abilities. For example, he told me that, while a patient of his had worked with numerous other therapists, "I was the only one who could help him." As well, he reported that he had to tell the patient's psychopharmacologist the correct diagnosis for the patient, thus

---

5. Ekstein and Wallerstein (1958) distinguished between "problems about learning" and "learning problems." The former are problems that arise for the supervisee in his work with his patient that are "projected onto the student's relationship with his supervisors" (p. 158); the latter are problems that occur in the therapeutic hour between supervisee and patient and are brought for discussion to the supervisor.

presenting himself as more knowledgeable than the psychiatrist. And these were just some aspects of his boastful,
self-aggrandizing presentation.

2. The supervisee's therapeutic stance was characterized by
an overly zealous desire to cure his patients. In his zeal, he
overidentified with the patients. Thus, when he presented
process notes on two quite different patients, they often
sounded similar to each other, even though they were diag-
nostically quite different. The supervisee's overidentification compromised his ability to understand and process
the patients' dynamics. It also prevented him from realisti-
cally assessing the possibilities and limitations of his therapeutic work (see Jacobs et al. 1995, p. 225).[6]

3. In presenting work in supervision, the supervisee presented himself as self-sufficient. Often, I had the feeling that
he wanted me, as his supervisor, to mirror his grandiosity.
He brought to mind a patient who had also presented as
though in her own cocoon (see Modell 1986). After many
years of analysis, the patient told me that, whenever I
pointed out something that hadn't already occurred to her,
she felt mortified. Because my insights made her feel criticized and belittled, she was unable to internalize my interpretations, thus negating much of our work together.

Like my patient, the supervisee was also in a cocoon,
presenting himself as needing no help. Since supervision
involves one person helping another, we were deadlocked:
How was I to teach someone who didn't appear to want to
be taught? One way I dealt with this deadlock was to ask
the supervisee, early in our work together, to think about
what he wanted to learn at this stage of his training. By

---

6. Overidentification might be a response to the supervisory relationship.
In addition to all its meanings with regard to the patient, it might serve as a
protective function for the supervisee vis-à-vis the supervisor.

asking him to define his learning needs, I was giving him a sense of control and autonomy.

While I believe that creating an explicit contract with the supervisee early in the supervision is important in all supervisory relationships (see Teitelbaum 1990), here it became a way of breaking through the supervisee's defensive armor and was crucial to establishing a learning alliance. In addressing the supervisee, I was careful about how to word my inquiries about his learning. For example, rather than asking, "What do you see as your needs, problems, or weaknesses?," I asked, "What do you understand to be your learning issues?" Among the questions I then had in mind were these: What would you like to get out of supervision? How will you communicate this to me? How do you feel you learn best? By staying away from phrasing that invoked needs and weakness and focusing on the supervision as a learning experience, I tried to free the supervisee from thinking in terms of dependency needs—a primary cause of his defensive stance. And, by highlighting the fact that this was a stage in the supervisee's development as a therapist, I credited him for all the work he had done up to this point, bolstering his shaky self-esteem.

CONCLUSION

Narcissistic vulnerability is an integral part of being a supervisee. The supervisee measures his experienced self against his ideal self, creating anxiety and inhibition in the supervisory relationship. This anxiety is compounded by the duality of roles and tasks required of the supervisee. In his dual role as the knowing therapist and the student seeking to learn, he must negotiate between conflicting self-representations. These factors contribute to the supervisee's inhibitions regarding self-exposure, particularly with regard to his personal feelings about his patients. It is important that the supervisor be aware of these vulnerabilities, and that he be particularly attentive to hidden or unconscious feelings the supervisee may have toward his patient so that they do not greatly hinder his professional growth. By assisting him in acknowledging and accepting these feelings (validation and normalizing), the supervisor helps bridge the gap between the supervisee's ideal self and his experienced self, thereby allowing the supervisee to work with fewer internal conflicts and inhibitions. With supervisees who exhibit narcissistic character defenses, extra effort must be made to engage them in the learning alliance. Empathy with the supervisee's fragile sense of self, and careful wording in defining his learning issues, can alleviate his fear of dependence on the supervisor, as well as loosen constricting internal ideals that deleteriously affect his self-esteem.

REFERENCES

Arkowitz, S. W. (1990). Perfectionism in the supervisee. *Psychoanalysis and Psychotherapy* 8:51–68.

Arlow, J. A. (1963). The supervisory situation. *Journal of the American Psychoanalytic Association* 11:576–594.

Brightman, B. K. (1984). Narcissistic issues in the training experience of the psychotherapist. *International Journal of Psychoanalytic Psychotherapy* 10:239–317.

Casement, P. (1991). *Learning from the Patient.* New York: Guilford.

Chasseguet-Smirgel, J. (1984). *The Ego Ideal.* New York: Norton.

Ekstein, R., and Wallerstein, R. S. (1958). *The Teaching and Learning of Psychotherapy.* New York: International Universities Press.

Epstein, L. (1986). Collusive selective inattention to the negative impact of the supervisory interaction. *Contemporary Psychoanalysis* 22:389–417.

Fleming, J., and Benedek, T. (1966). *Psychoanalytic Supervision: A Method of Clinical Teaching.* New York: Grune & Stratton.

Ford, E. S. C. (1963). Being and becoming a psychotherapist: the search for identity. *American Journal of Psychotherapy* 17:472–482.

Freud, S. (1914). On narcissism: an introduction. *Standard Edition* 14:67–107.

Glickauf-Hughes, C. (1994). Characterological resistances in psychotherapy supervision. *Psychotherapy* 31:58–66.

Jacobs, D., David, P., and Meyer, D. (1995). *The Supervisory Encounter.* New Haven: Yale University Press.

Jacobson, E. (1964). *The Self and the Object World.* New York: International Universities Press.

Mehlman, R. D. (1974). Becoming and being a psychotherapist. *International Journal of Psychoanalytic Psychotherapy* 3:125–141.

Modell, A. (1975). A narcissistic defense against affects and the illusion of self-sufficiency. In *Essential Papers on Narcissism,* ed. A. P. Morrison, pp. 293–307. New York: New York University Press, 1986.

———. (1993). *The Private Self.* Cambridge: Harvard University Press.

Morrison, A. P. (1983). Shame, ideal self, and narcissism. In *Essential Papers on Narcissism,* ed. A. P. Morrison, pp. 348–371. New York: New York University Press, 1986.

Rangell, L. (1969). The intrapsychic process and its analysis: a recent life of thought and its current implications. *International Journal of Psycho-Analysis* 50:65–77.

Rock, M. H., ed. (1997). Effective supervision. In *Psychodynamic Supervision: Perspectives of the Supervisor and the Supervisee,* pp. 107–132. Northvale, NJ: Jason Aronson.

Sandler, J., Holder, A., and Meers, D. (1963). The ego ideal and the ideal self. *Psychoanalytic Study of the Child* 18:139–158. New York: International Universities Press.

Schafer, R. (1967). Ideals, the ego ideal, and the ideal self. *Psychological Issues* 5:131–174.

Searles, H. (1962). Problems of psycho-analytic supervision. In *Collected Papers on Schizophrenia and Related Subjects,* pp. 584–604. New York: International Universities Press, 1965.

Sharaf, M. R., and Levinson, D. J. (1964). The quest for omnipotence in professional training. *Psychiatry* 27:135–149.

Stolorow, R., Atwood, G., and Brandchaft, B. (1994). *The Intersubjective Perspective*. Northvale, NJ: Jason Aronson.

Teitelbaum, S. H. (1990). Aspects of the contract in psychotherapy supervision. *Psychoanalysis and Psychotherapy* 8:95–98.

Tischler, G. L. (1968). The beginning resident and supervision. *Archives of General Psychiatry* 19:418–422.

Winnicott, D. W. (1960). The theory of the patient–infant relationship. In *The Maturational Processes and the Facilitating Environment*, pp. 37–55. New York: International Universities Press, 1965.

3

Perfectionism in the Supervisee

SYDNEY W. ARKOWITZ

Over a period of teaching and supervising psychoanalytic psychotherapy, I have observed how frequently supervisees' perfectionistic strivings become central in the learning process and development of professional identity. In some respects these strivings can aid in mastery. However, they frequently form a core of difficulties, impeding learning and professional development. Sometimes there is a fine line between striving for perfection and striving for excellence, and it is not always clear where one stops and the other begins. In fact, perfectionism could be thought of as a distortion of the normal strivings for mastery and competence that go on throughout adult as well as child development.

By perfectionism, here, I am referring to a deleterious phenomenon with regard to the effect on mastery, in this case, of therapeutic principles and processes, and on self-esteem. Central to this phenomenon is the denial or disavowal of significant aspects of inner and outer reality.

When self-esteem is based on standards that are harsh and highly exacting, failure to meet them leads to self-denigration and self-mortification, as self-accusations take place that are out of proportion to external reality. The same harsh standards are also applied to others. The holding of unrealistic goals, lying within the domain of the ego ideal, applies to both action and feeling. Brightman (1984) has postulated a common constellation among trainees of a grandiose self consisting of omniscience, benevolence, and omnipotence. My experience with supervisees is that many think they should be able to fix the unfixable, know the unknowable, and love the unlovable. Defensive operations against the narcissistic injuries this perpetuates then add a dimension of confusion to the picture.

Perfectionism also stands in the way of mastery and spontaneity of self-expression, which is crucial to mastery of psychoanalytic treatment, as the use of the self is central to it. Standards of excellence, which in themselves may be pertinent, can be rigidly exacting according to narrow dimensions. As such, the degree of attentiveness to them that is required is so great that important aspects of relevant reality are missed. The dimensions of what the individual has identified as important then seem to be everything that is important, so that they are out of proportion to the work as a whole. The organization of the perceptual field is distorted, as for example, when the supervisee is empathic to a patient's early trauma, while ignoring the patient's rage and her own counterreaction of rage.

PERFECTIONISM IN THE SUPERVISORY SITUATION

Perfectionistic strivings are heightened in supervision because vulnerability is heightened. This is due to the transitional nature of the supervisee's professional identity, whether novice or experienced. Also, the supervisory situation itself contains factors that fan perfectionism. These arise deeply from both superego dictates and unresolved issues of omnipotence or, as McDougall (1985) has put it, from the domains of the Forbidden and the Impossible.

As in any transitional position, new solutions are not yet clear. Supervisees new to the process of psychoanalytic therapy have more intellectual knowledge than they know what to do with. Information about themselves, others, and the process float in and out of awareness with minimal integration. With more experience, the deepening appreciation of the perplexities of being human and of the psychoanalytic process itself raises at least as many questions as it answers. Unknowns seem to multiply, leading to anxiety, then to an intensification of a wish for definite answers. Old superego dictates of right and wrong rigidify in an attempt to respond to this need. Thrown off balance by the confrontation with the limits of their knowledge, they lose perspective on what is enough knowledge, trying also to regain balance in a struggle toward omniscience.

In the ever-evolving nature of professional identity, there is a perpetual state of transition, hand-in-hand with structural reorganization. For change, we depend on new identifications as well as analysis and synthesis of experience. Both take place in supervision as well. As in any process where this is happening, confusion and anxiety about change itself are stimulated through fear of the unknown. This then intensifies as new identifications conflict with old ones and as internal reorganization is unstable (Kennedy and Yorke 1982, Loewald 1980).

In response, there tends to be a forward and backward motion, as supervisees question what to trust. Alternatively, they welcome the expansion of the new, then rigidify what has worked in the past. With the uncertainty of their position, they are pressured to deal in some way with their own limitations. Lifelong methods of avoiding narcissistic wounds and emotional vulnerability come into play. Ironically, to do psychoanalytically oriented treatment, we must permit emotional vulnerability, allowing the patient's person to impact on our own. Caught between the threats that vulnerability entails and the need to allow it for the work, beginning supervisees particularly are pressured toward a perfectionistic constriction. This sometimes alternates with overactivity, as they try to fix things, a role they are likely to have played in the past.

Supervisors, too, have an ever-evolving professional identity. However, theirs is likely to be more firmly established. It is hoped that this enables them to view the supervisee with an empathic and balanced perspective.

The supervisory relationship, while intended to augment learning in a safe context, itself stimulates uncertainty, vulnerability, and regression. First, new supervisees are struggling to understand what is expected of them, not only in their role as therapist, but as supervisee as well, where it is even less clear. If they are in therapy or analysis, this along with didactics provides some sense of who they will become as therapists, but there is no preparation for who they are in the supervisory relationship. They look to the supervisor for what is expected here as well as what to do in the treatment. They hope for clear guidelines to these two elusive endeavors, for standards of right and wrong, when such standards become foggier the more they are examined. They often emerge from such encounters even more confused.

Second, the demands of the learning situation include the stress from a need to adapt repeatedly to the differential demands of three kinds of relationships: as therapist, as supervisee, and as patient. In their role as therapist, supervisees are more in charge of the definition of the relationship, where they reveal less of themselves than do patients and where they set the structure. In their own treatment, this is reversed, as it is in supervision. It is likely that those of us who choose this profession enjoy the kind of protection that comes with the role of therapist, for varying dynamic reasons. To then be the more vulnerable one, as supervisee and patient, brings a movement toward regression, as control lessens.

The learning process itself requires a certain regression. Where old knowledge conflicts with new knowledge, it must be questioned, and the process of integrating new knowledge lacks stability. Then, in this uncertain state, because psychotherapy relies so heavily on the self as an instrument, there is a need for self-exposure as well, at the same time as there is a drop in healthy narcissism.

All of this leads to increased dependency on the supervisor for help. This position tends to be conflictually held, with elements of fear and relief, for the supervisor potentially judges as much as supports and validates. Where idealizations of the supervisor involve competitive feelings of inadequacy or the need to please, insecurity with the supervisor is fostered at the same time the supervisor is so needed. In treatment, there is an opportunity to deal with these responses and this is, in fact, central to it. This is not, however, the aim of supervision, where the heightened vulnerability itself is likely to increase the expectation of being judged. In order to avoid and master this painfully passive position, attempts to do the judging oneself are stimulated, either of oneself, the supervisor, or the patient.

In addition, it has been suggested that many therapists' early dependent relationships have been disappointing, and that the ego ideal has then come to consider it more acceptable to be needed than to need (Miller 1981, Searles 1975). Superego dictates, elaborating on this, forbid regressive attachments as wrong, as well as dangerous. Such strictures are likely to intensify in proportion to the arousal of regression and dependency.

Where perfectionistic strivings are stimulated in substitution for examination of anxiety, they express, in a sense, the wish to not know and to be unknowable. They serve as attempts to control through avoiding the regressive threats in the learning situation and the supervisory relationship, as well as to impose a form of structure in the elusive processes of supervision and psychotherapy. In this, they interfere with both treatment and learning. They function much in the way inner conflict does: inhibiting awareness, expression, and action or forcing a compromise solution in a distorted expression.

For example, fear of making an error leads to various kinds of freezing. Often this takes the form of blocking attunement to one's self during the session, so that there is a shrinkage in richness of feeling and fantasy. Sometimes thought and fantasy are there, but the ability to make an intervention is blocked, as the supervisee-therapist rejects possibilities as not good enough. Another form of blockage occurs when fears of supervisor judgment lead to difficulties in remembering the session.

For some, the need to be perfect results not so much in inhibitions as in pressure to make something happen. For them, it is difficult to be at ease with the position of passive activity, and they tread on the patient's territory, interfering with the unfolding process and the emerging person of the patient.

Both inhibitions and excesses are also obviously dynamic expressions of the supervisee. Forbidden sexual or aggressive wishes, the need to subjugate one's needs to those of others, rescue fantasies as reaction formations and reparative wishes central to one's identity, and fear of passive wishes are but a few. While these clearly must be dealt with through exploration in depth in the supervisee's own treatment, their painful manifestations in the supervisee's work, fanned as they are by the demands of the learning situation, become a challenge of supervision.

To the extent that perfectionistic constellations, woven in a developmental matrix of unresolved grandiosity, an unrealistic ego ideal, and harsh superego structures, form a core of difficulties in the learning and doing of psychotherapy, supervision inevitably becomes a kind of developmental challenge.

The early debates about the nature of supervision, originating in whether it should be an extension of personal analysis or not, revolved around defining supervision as limited to a training aimed at increased skill or a broader definition, focusing on the development of professional identity. These debates seem to have been largely settled in favor of the latter, as more recent work, focusing on phenomena such as parallel process, countertransference, and the learning alliance, demonstrates (Caligor 1981, Doehrman 1976, Ekstein and Wallerstein 1958, Fleming and Benedek 1966, Gediman and Wolkenfeld 1980, Goin and Kline 1976, Grinberg 1979, Lakovics 1983, Lowrer 1972, Lubin 1984).

In this chapter, my emphasis is on the contributions possible through supervision toward a modification of the supervisee's ego ideal, softening of superego structures, and increasing relinquishment of grandiosity and the attainment of realistic confidence in one's experience. Such structural developments are core to the evolution of professional identity. With this, there is an impact on the development of greater empathy and authenticity, of increased breadth and depth in the use of the self as an instrument of treatment, and of appreciation of the multidimensional nature of human experience. When supervision is considered, as it is here, central to the development of identity, rather than as the acquisition of knowledge and skill alone, its definition becomes more complicated. First, the goals become those of some degree of structural change. As such, the processes in supervision are psychoanalytic ones, namely, identification, analysis, and synthesis. In addition, parameters involving a challenge to ego development through direct exercise of ego functions are also involved.

However, with these fundamentals of change basic to both processes, it also becomes important to clarify the differences between them. Both psychotherapy and supervision aim at increased mastery, the development of curiosity and creative ability, and the development of the ability to be the source of self-knowledge. However, as others have pointed out (Doehrman 1976, Ekstein and Wallerstein 1958, Fleming and Benedek 1966), the aim in treatment is the use of the self in life as a whole, while in supervision it is the use of the self as it relates to doing treatment and to studying personality. As such, the supervisory process is deep; at the same time it is more limited in scope. For the supervisor, the challenge becomes how to use clinical understanding and skill within this differently defined context.

Thus, supervision should not be the same as treatment, nor can it be. Because evaluation of the supervisee is part of the structure of the process, the specific goals cannot be completely negotiated, as they are in psychotherapy. In addition, the supervisor's judging function automatically provides some degree of inhibition to the fullest expression and exploration of the issues. To try to make supervision into treatment is to undermine the real reasons for being there. Furthermore, it confuses the definition of the working relationship, inevitably leading to anxiety and hostility. In such cases, it is not uncommon for the supervisee to develop excessive criticalness, overtly or perhaps covertly withdrawing from the supervisor. While such a stance is frequently seen as indicative of supervisee problems, this may be not only an expression of hostility, but an attempt to reestablish the boundaries that have been loosened through confusing the definition of the relationship. Such a development, while expressing in part perfectionistic demands turned on the supervisor, is an expression of the supervisee's need for structure. In fact, constellations of perfectionistic strivings in general, as attempts to reduce anxiety by establishing control, speak to the need for more workable forms of containment and mastery, since these strivings lead to further problems. This need is greater in supervision than in therapy. Addressing it begins with the structure provided through the definition of the supervisory situation.

THE STRUCTURE OF THE SUPERVISORY SPACE

The delicacy of this task is that there is a need not only for boundaries, but also for their permeability and for open space. We want to teach what we know, to facilitate the expression of individuality in the supervisee's professional development, and to combine clear expectations with open exploration, toward the integration of these facets of learning and development.

Toward these ends, Winnicott's (1958b) work on transitional processes is pertinent: "No human being is free from the strain of relating inner and outer reality. Relief from this strain is provided by an intermediate area of experience that is not challenged" (p. 240), an area that lies between the inability and the ability to accept reality. Without this, there would be no creativity. The adaptation to reality would be flat and colorless.

Within the supervisory situation, the supervisees' inner reality can be thought of as everything they bring to the learning situation, their old ways of perceiving, feeling, and acting. External reality then becomes everything that stems from their interactions with their patient and supervisor, and to some extent with the training institution, particularly what is new. Supervisees negotiate the relationship between these two realities by singling out elements and integrating them, by exploring them in their individual ways. Thus, they create their own rendition of meaning of these new experiences—their personal reality. This grows out of the intermediate area of experience Winnicott (1958b) talks about, an area of open possibilities. As an area that is unchallenged, it is free of judgment and thus free of perfectionistic strivings. Supervisors must allow for this area of potential space. More than that, they must expect it, so that the supervisees will come to expect it as well. As such, this draws direct attention to the inevitability and the necessity of uncertainty and of regression, both in the service of the ego and in the creation of meaning. Supervision then also becomes a forum for the dilemmas and conflicts about the supervisees' identity in transition. In this way, ongoing goals of separation-individuation are facilitated, expanding the professional self and allowing for autonomy and competence to be increasingly exchanged for omnipotence (for discussions of the relationship of transitional processes and the use of space in development, see Bergman 1978, Deri 1978).

The how-to's of facilitating this process come into focus. They rest on providing a structure compatible with the analytic process, through boundary establishment and permeability. Such a structure requires a balance of closed or protected space and open or generative space. As supervisors negotiate this, their own version of the strain in relating inner and outer reality could be thought of as coalescing in the need to traverse between the dangers of intrusion or abandonment with respect to the supervisees.

I would like to propose the following in response to the need to structure the supervisory space. I suggest that this space, determined as it is by its aims, needs an organizing focus for them, the use of clinical tools, and attention to phenomena in the supervisory and treatment processes (for example, parallel process and countertransference). Further, all of this occurs within the context of the supervisory working relationship and through the medium of language.

ORGANIZING FOCUS: SUPERVISOR AND SUPERVISEE

I propose the organizing focus be overt, through a repeatedly returning attention to the supervisees' experience of the patient and the treatment as well as of the supervisor and the supervisory relationship, given that the aims are for supervisees to learn about themselves in both contexts. At the same time, core to this organizing focus, though not always overtly addressed, is the supervisor defined in ways specific to the emphasis here.

Whatever their meanings are to the supervisees, which may be many, supervisors serve as a referent, with respect to which the supervisees define and redefine themselves. As such, this process parallels parameters developed in psychoanalytic psychotherapy, which rely on growth through the active challenge to ego functions when therapists integrate their own reactions into interventions. In addition, the supervisor also is almost always initially a superego representative, often idealized, but certainly experienced as a judge. Thus, perfection is unconsciously held as attainable, and the search for it begins with the supervisor as the referent.

In order to move toward modification of supervisee perfectionism, the supervisor can become a referent that represents a different kind of ego ideal, one that recognizes that perfection forever eludes us. As such, alternative values to the attainment of perfection are needed within this ego ideal. First is replacement by a value on completion. By completion I mean the identification and integration of whatever elements of experience are available at the moment. The significance of this is that what is complete at one point in time inevitably becomes incomplete at another, so that the meaning of completion constantly shifts. There is never a final completion; there are segments of completion, then linkages and reorganization among the segments. Thus, while perfection represents a static state, completion, as defined here, represents motion. A value on process replaces a value on product. Paralleling the analytic process itself, this acknowledges the ongoing nature of development, the individuality of experience, and that answers to questions of existence eventually lead to more questions. This acknowledgment leads to more adaptive and creative resolutions. The enactment of such a value in supervision lies in the supervisor's fluid attention within this learning situation, returning repeatedly to the supervisee's experience as the organizing focus.

Also, in fostering a move away from perfectionism as a value, the supervisor's willingness to be imperfect is crucial. First, this means tolerating the limits of what we can give, for example, as indicated in a supervisee's dissatisfaction with a particular supervisory session. It also means acknowledging mistakes or having missed something, either in the material presented or in the supervisee's response to us.

Second, this means tolerating the ambiguities in both the therapy and supervisory situations. Our willingness to use our responses in pursuing paths of uncertainty as well as feelings a supervisee finds unacceptable, such as, "I'm confused," or, "Something doesn't fit here," or, "I seem to both like and dislike this patient, though I don't know why," or, "If I were in your shoes, I think I'd hate that patient," speaks to the inevitability of ambiguity and touches on the equal inevitability of ambivalence and presence of hate, anger, and love in response to those we wish to help, as well as love, concern, and empathy.

As supervisors, we have the privilege to expose more of ourselves than we do as therapists, which also means we are more vulnerable. Although vulnerability is often perceived as a weakness, indicating imperfection, the use of our vulnerabilities within the supervisory relationship is central to the ego ideal we represent (for discussions of supervisor reactions, see Allphin 1987,

Searles 1965a,b). It is our vulnerability, really our ability to respond emotionally to others, that is so valuable in a growing understanding of them. As increasing elements of experience are permitted exposure, analysis, and synthesis, there is a growing appreciation of individuality of experience and style, as we recognize, supervisor and supervisee, our unique vulnerabilities in relating to the material the supervisee presents and within the context of our interactions about it.

In representing this alternative ego ideal, our aim is not to directly de-idealize ourselves, as often the need to idealize temporarily stems from a developmental process (see Kohut 1971, on selfobject needs) [Rather, our aim is to demonstrate that something valuable comes from vulnerability and that we find out something through not knowing]

This, then, is one way the supervisor becomes a referent, through representing the kind of ego ideal defined here. The supervisor thus serves as an organizer covertly, as an undercurrent. I suggest the overt organizing principle be a repeatedly returning focus on the way the supervisee experiences the work of both therapy and supervision. While the need to enter the inner world of the supervisee has been pointed out (Arlow 1963, Fleming and Benedek 1966, Muslin and Val 1980), I am suggesting here that this entrance provides the focal point of organization, for the following reasons.

First, the best thing we can teach is probably how to use the self as a source of information, how to tune into oneself and one's patients. Second, it is only the supervisee who is in direct contact with the other two—the patient and the supervisor. Because of this, differences with respect to the patient cannot be negotiated without first understanding the supervisee's version of what happened and her reasons for interventions. Last, if the supervisee's self-esteem is ignored, we will get nowhere.

This focus does not mean probing into the supervisee. For example, an initial focus on the supervisee's perceptions of the patient allows a kind of testing ground, where both these perceptions, with their uncertainties, and the patient with her vulnerabilities, can be experienced as acceptable to the supervisor. This then paves the way for supervisees to be accepting as well, so that they can then talk more directly and freely about themselves, their sources of difficulty, and their pride in the learning and doing of psychotherapy (Epstein 1986).

Central to the focus on the supervisees and fostering of the flexibility we value is an appreciation of their natural capacities and learning styles, also involving vulnerability. Work begun by Ekstein and Wallerstein (1958) emphasizes that the supervisee learns through resolving problems in his learning. In addition to the resistances to learning, caused by inevitable conflicts about change and receiving help, there are conflict-free areas, as well as creative translations in the absorption and integration of new information. Furthermore, the conflicts themselves, managed in individual ways, often have imaginative resolutions, combining positive with negative features and perhaps representing a more general and ubiquitous balance of destructive and constructive forces.

For example, a tendency to handle supervision with debate may reflect a need to define oneself through saying no, but it may also be a primary tool for a kind of trial action that is a way to learn. Engaging in this way in fact often helps clarify ideas and challenges the supervisor to rethink issues. Such can also be the case with some intellectualized supervisees. A highly cerebral approach to emotion, transforming emotion into ideas, may be a device to ward off feeling. However, this approach may also protect a wish to feel and may be used to approach feelings cautiously, as the supervisee tries to become familiar with feelings by using means that provide some comfort. The caution in such style would be respected, for when individuals are able to meet their own need to exercise control, to regulate the pace of the process so as not to feel overwhelmed or invalidated, they are also better able to learn. We must also, of course, address learning problems and problems in learning (see Chapter 2, note 5, this volume). Open discussions are acceptances of problems, representing our expectations of imperfection and vulnerability. However, if we can first accept the positive side of the supervisees' efforts, they are more likely to expose their uncertainties in the service of the supervisory work. Then, in addition to an exploration of their capacities, there can also be an exploration of how painful or limiting their learning styles may be. While this in itself may be painful, a growing awareness of how they negotiate gaps in their knowledge leads to more knowledge and the security that comes from it.

Our ability to allow our supervisees the freedom to develop their own way of using us respects their contribution to the definition of the relationship. It also honors the fact that there is more than one way to move toward a goal. Supervisees' self-acceptance increases through confidence in their autonomy, expressed through their individual ways of doing, as well as through their growing self-knowledge. Such knowledge, being a source of realistic pride and thus a more serviceable form of control in its mastery, then mutes the perfectionistic strivings that have also aimed at control and mastery.

CLINICAL TOOLS

The clinical tools pertinent here rest on the empathic stance that is always at the core of our work. They are: to draw out what is in the supervisee; to use our own responses in clarifying what belongs to whom in the therapy and supervisory relationships; and to return to the significance of these discoveries for the treatment itself.

By drawing out what is in the supervisee with regard to the patient (i.e., countertransference, identifications, visual and verbal associations to patient productions, interventions and the pride or shame associated with them, fears resulting in inhibited or overactive interventions) and to the supervisor (i.e., differences of perception and opinion, misunderstandings in communication, empathic failures, rejection of supervisor input), we are of course teaching the therapeutic process. However, in addition, we address fears of being judged, self-judgments, and judgments of others, providing an opportunity for a degree of reorganization of such a constellation, as it is identified in some detail. When this pursuit is empathic and respectful, curiosity is stimulated, and a growing pleasure in discovery can increasingly replace the monitoring of what is right or wrong, which inhibits open investigation.

For example, a supervisee presented work with a patient who took an intimidated stance toward her mother. I asked what she thought the intimidation was about, and she found herself blocked in exploring this, as she was with her patient as well. She easily recognized her identification with the patient and was surprised when I asked if she thought she might be like the mother as well. She said, "No," then, "Actually, I'd hate to be like her. She's a terrible person—so critical." As she realized that she, too, was criticizing, she then became afraid I would criticize her in turn. Recognizing this spiraling constellation led her to a fuller access to other feelings as well, and then to be less inhibited and tense with her patient.

Probably the most important thing we teach is how we arrive at formulations through tuning in to ourselves and our patient in the moment-to-moment shifts, for it is in this way that autonomous assessments of what matters are made[Identifying the elements of experience and understanding their meanings enhance more realistic sources of control through mastery] Obviously, it is easier to deal with something that has shape and is in focus than something that is vague and blurry. As clear recognitions of one's experiences are attained, fantasy is replaced by personal reality. Thus, the supervisees' confidence in their fluctuating feelings and associations and their value increases. They can then begin to integrate the inner reality of their own experience with the outer reality of the patients' productions, forming hypotheses of meaning for pursuit. What initially may appear as generated by magic omniscience when watching an experienced therapist or analyst at work now becomes more ordinary and knowable. In this, secondary narcissism increasingly replaces primary narcissism, and the perfectionism of omnipotence abates.

In learning to attend fluidly to moment-to-moment shifts, the supervisee develops an ability to suspend judgment in making transitory and fluctuating identifications with the patient and the figures in the patient's life. As this parallels what the supervisor is doing with the supervisee and the patient, the supervisee is thus internalizing new identifications with the learning process itself. The supervisor further facilitates growth by clarifying what belongs to whom in the therapy and supervisory relationships. Given that conflict and defense always exist in patient, supervisee, and supervisor alike, this can be a complicated task. In addition, the complex processes we are trying to articulate are often transpiring at nonverbal levels. In this form, they perhaps express a need to have others feel what we feel without words. When doing therapy, we carefully weigh what to do when we recognize our feelings as reverberations of our patients' inner lives. As supervisors, we can more freely share our own experience directly, in order to discover what belongs to whom. We can sort out together the source and meaning of each of our thoughts, feelings, and fantasies. A fragment of an example follows.

> A supervisee presented his frustration with a seeming impasse of therapy. His presentation had a stalemate quality. I thought, there must be something else as well, and felt an uneasy helplessness, which I expressed to him. Pondering this, he said my reaction alerted him to a sense of something else, too, and then he remembered the patient smiling "strangely." The patient, he realized, had reminded him at that moment of a baby just waking. He then smiled himself, in a way that seemed to be blissful. I pointed this out. As he seemed to have trouble exploring this, I told him also of a reaction I had had, of feeling excluded when he smiled. He chuckled, surprised, and said, actually there was a certain pleasure in things just as they were with this patient. Was this, he asked, what a mother feels in that period of normal symbiosis Mahler describes?

With this kind of careful attention, the delineation between the emotional forces of all three of us became sharper. With this thread in the work made visible, the supervisee's trust in his own perceptions and intuition was enhanced, and the appreciation of the fluidity of experience was heightened, modifying the ego ideal and enhancing the value of process.

Always, then, directing what has been discovered back to the meaning for the patient and the treatment not only teaches through demonstration, but respects boundaries through preservation of the definition of the relationship as a supervisory one. This fluid movement between supervisee and patient, between supervisee and supervisor, always returning to the significance for the treatment, illustrates and exercises both elasticity and establishment of boundaries. Thus, in the above example, once the supervisee wondered about normal symbiosis, the pleasure he seemed to be experiencing also seemed to evaporate, and he said he did not feel very comfortable. I asked what was uncomfortable. He said that these feelings weren't very masculine. I asked if there was anything else, feeling again the presence of something additional. He said that actually, he had first had a fleeting thought that I had told him of a feeling of helplessness on my part, and then the other thought about masculinity had flashed. We discussed this in regard to both of us and then wondered together what these feelings might be saying about the patient.

Without using these discoveries to return to the meaning for the patient, formlessness would ensue, and the supervisee would be left to flounder or rigidify as he tried to figure out what was expected of him.

If the supervisor is unable to represent alternative ego ideals to perfection, to establish boundaries through the framework of the supervisory relationship and work, or to focus on the meaning of the work to the supervisee, various problems ensue. In continuing to strive for perfection through the maintenance of an idealization of the supervisor that remains unchallenged, supervisees may also fail to challenge the supervisor and may even attribute their own qualities to the supervisor. If supervisors are unable to be imperfect and vulnerable but are clear about what they expect, supervisees may focus primarily on pleasing the supervisor according to the supervisor's criteria, at the expense of developing their own unique potential. If supervisors are not clear about what they expect, or if they fail to clearly define the supervisory relationship, supervisees may turn their perfectionism toward excessive criticalness of the supervisor in an attempt to establish boundaries. If supervisors are not attuned to the supervisees' experience, common when concern is greater for the patient than for the supervisee, the supervisees may develop a need to ward off the supervisor. This also happens when the supervisor supervises through a heavy use of countertransference interpretations of supervisee unresolved conflict.

THE PHENOMENA TAUGHT: PSYCHOTHERAPY AND SUPERVISION

The teaching of psychotherapy in supervision has been identified as directed primarily at countertransference in therapy and parallel process of therapy and supervision (Ekstein and Wallerstein 1958, Gediman and Wolkenfeld 1980, Goin and Kline 1976). Both rest on a temporary weakening and permeability of boundaries. To the extent that the regressions involved stimulate fears of being judged by the supervisor or violate the supervisee's own criteria for self-esteem, this contributes to the tightening of defenses that often coalesce in perfectionist strivings.

Both countertransference and parallel process illustrate how intrapsychic processes have a life of their own, that they simply are not under our control. The supervisee is repeatedly faced with this, and forced to deal with both it and the supervisor's limitations and vulnerabilities. This ongoing process then is a developmental task, or crisis, in coming to terms with the inevitable failure of omnipotence and omniscience. Brightman (1984) suggests this kind of crisis in professional development relates to training as a whole and necessitates a professional mourning process.

The difficulty beginning supervisees have in appreciating the value of countertransference in understanding our patients is heavily related to this crisis, as they often feel they should not be experiencing countertransference. This leads then to frustration, anger, fear, and self-blame, which trigger attempts to distance from the patient and then from the supervisor.

The experience of parallel process now actively engages the supervisor as well, as the complexity of forces multiplies exponentially. All three participants play both initiating and responding roles, mirroring or complementing the others (Racker 1957), and in defense against emerging conflict. The understanding of parallel process as it has evolved is that it is based on similarities with the repetition compulsion, namely, that what is not understood is enacted (Bromberg 1982, Caligor 1981, Doehrman 1976, Ekstein and Wallerstein 1958, Gediman and Wolkenfeld 1980). I would like to emphasize the aim of mastery here. Enactments are dramatizations, magnifications that provide an opportunity to see what is more clearly. They may also express a wish to be understood without words. Supervisees bring to us this problem through their role in the parallel process. It is important to appreciate that there is a wish for help and for mastery and to acknowledge this.

For example, a new supervisee reported a therapy with a patient who felt overwhelmed by intense affects. The supervisee found himself anxious in the sessions and troubled by dreams that seemed to reflect the patient's intensity. Through supervision, he came to realize the patient wanted to get rid of her intense feelings by giving them to him. He then proceeded to tell her that he could understand her wish, but that he couldn't do this for her, that perhaps they could think of ways to control her feelings. He told me that he was pleased he was able to not do what she wanted, as it had always been a problem for him to say no to people. He then said, with great feeling, that he thought he really needed to talk about himself rather than his patient. I now found myself challenged to find a way to redefine the work as supervision rather than as therapy, which could duplicate his clamping down on his patient.

This supervisee, frightened by his patient's intensities and uncertain of his ability to manage them, was trying to deny where he had a responsibility to choose instead the role of patient. With the patient, he was prohibiting an expression of intensity; with me he was asking to express intensity. In this, he was turning the problem of how to manage intensity, so that it could be examined from different perspectives. This then, was an attempt at mastery. All of this needed to be addressed, including the positive aspects of his struggle.

Through the supervisor's open use of her responses in parallel process, supervisees begin to see they are not alone, that the supervisor is vulnerable as well to countertransference, projective identification, transitory identifications, and failures of empathy. These discoveries often lead initially to a disappointment in the supervisor, which must then be dealt with. With this, progress is made toward the relinquishment of the omnipotent wishes that cause so much difficulty. The ability to negotiate this successfully also leads to supervisees feeling that they remain in good company; the realization of the supervisor's similar vulnerabilities to intrapsychic processes is normalizing. At the same time, the supervisor's ability to deal with them with an empathic, respectful approach provides a standard of excellence.

Within the intimate nature of the work, supervisees must face the inevitability of ambivalence, their reactions of hate as well as love, the presence of destructive as well as constructive forces, and the realization that we are all vehicles for one another's inner worlds. At the same time, aided by the supervisor's attention to their areas that are conflict-free as well as conflicted, to their imaginative use of transitional processes, and to their wish for mastery, supervisees acquire an increasing depth of knowledge. They also create their own applications of that knowledge, so that secondary narcissism replaces primary narcissism.

Common fears emerge among supervisees, related deeply to the intrapsychic conflict imbedded in this material. Fear of invading the patient usually combines conflict about aggression with a sensitivity to the intrusive potential of interpretation. Another is fear of causing undue dependency, reflecting conflict about dependency, stirred in the supervisory relationship to it, including confusion about the relationship of dependency and autonomy. A third is of intense feelings, reflecting deeper fears of regression, fanned too by the regression in the supervisory relationship. While these issues can only be fully explored in the supervisees' own treatment, they occur so routinely that the identification of them within the supervisory encounter tends to have a normalizing effect, paving the way for permission to feel whatever it is one feels and the freedom to use that to understand the patient.

In addition, multitudinal elements become clearer: their identifications and defenses against them; their existing resolutions to being helped and giving help, touching on the relationship to deeper issues of dependency; their existing resolutions to changing and facilitating change; their way of associating to patient productions; their fear, guilt, and pride in making particular interventions.

To the degree that conflicted and nonconflicted material is increasingly identified, some degree of structural reorganization begins to take place, with implications for a more workable relationship of superego to ego. Self-differentiation also is furthered (Mahler et al. 1975), with widening possibilities for full and authentic self-representation in the therapeutic process.

It has been noted that the phenomena of parallel process continue to surprise us. The following is an example of this for me, under somewhat unusual circumstances.

A supervisee with a background in research and behavioral approaches to psychotherapy was in supervision and seminars with me for a limited period, due to the nature of his training. He had a flair for facilitating group discussions and ameliorating conflict. He engaged intellectually openly and with imagination, interested in the new ideas in my different theoretical framework. He frequently developed others' thoughts in new ways. There was a marked contrast to the vitality in intellectual exchange with him and the general evenness of his emotional tone, always considerate, with me, his patient, and the seminar participants. Occasionally, he was a bit ruffled by something I said, generally in pointing to what I thought his experience was with his patient. He would then ponder what I had said, but seemed a bit defensive.

Several months into supervision, he uncharacteristically complained about one of the seminar members. He became uncomfortable about criticizing his colleague, and this led to my telling him that although we exchanged our thoughts about his patient, theoretical systems, and psychotherapy, I rarely knew what anything meant to him. He said feelings did seem to make him uncomfortable, but he thought he was doing better. He then gave several examples as "proof," and it was apparent he was struggling to evaluate these. During the six months of supervision, I did not think he had opened very much to his experience of things, although he had managed to provide enough availability to his patient that she was able to discover, to a degree, the anger behind her depression.

When we were saying goodbye, I meant to tell him that I hoped to follow his career. As I was doing so, to my surprise, I started to cry, so I stopped what I was saying and told him I would miss him. Not at all uncomfortable, he jumped out of his chair, hugged me, and said that having me for a teacher had meant a great deal to him. As I regained a sense of balance, I said that my tears had totally taken me by surprise, and that I thought I was probably doing the crying for both of us. He responded with his usual sparkle of interest at a new idea, and said that maybe I was right. He then referred to the time I had told him I did not know what things meant to him, that it had made him nervous, he did not want this kind of supervision, but he had found himself thinking about it ever since, and that perhaps he would go into therapy. I am sure all of this impacted on me as much as on him.

Later, I watched a videotape I had made of a supervision session with him, in which the patient talked about fishing, throwing out the line and taking it in, over and over. In the tape, I pointed out how she was having difficulty letting him in and often shut him out, also that he seemed frustrated. He became defensive, saying this used to be true. Once I was able to acknowledge the way he saw these changes, he then was able to consider what I had observed. Only after watching this tape did I realize how much the metaphor of the fishing line had been going on during the entire six months.

THE CONTEXT: THE WORKING RELATIONSHIP

The context of the supervisory work, the working relationship, itself is an unfolding process, one of trial and error, of fumbling, of mutual adaptation, all aimed at maximizing learning. The way this is worked out, including impasses, again is distinctive to the individual personalities. Doehrman (1976) concludes from ongoing interviews of supervisors and supervisees that how well the impasses are worked out is in part a function of how clearly the transferences involved are recognized. Awareness of what it takes and willingness to do so set a standard of excellence in the midst of uncertainty and fallibility.

To negotiate a learning alliance in this context means for supervisors that we must understand the way the supervisee experiences us. For example, I tend to use emotionally charged words to help supervisees attune to disavowed aspects of feelings. I have found some respond to this as permission to feel, while others are uncomfortable and become more defensive. I have also come to recognize that differing constellations of dynamics develop between us, as wishes and conflicts on both our parts come into play. When my method is not experienced by the new supervisee as facilitative, I usually note this and do it less, if not drop it all together. Open discussions are not always helpful early in the relationship. Often, this is as in treatment, where transference is not typically addressed until the patient has tested the therapist's trustworthiness in the patient's unique ways. In supervision, this generally revolves around whether the supervisor cares, understands, appreciates, and respects the supervisee, and whether the supervisor is someone the supervisee can admire and respect as a clinician. With some supervisees, open discussion of the supervisory relationship early on enhances trust. The individuality in the way each supervisory pair moves toward trust again illustrates that there is no one right way, but many.

In an example of my experience negotiating a working relationship, I initially felt shut out by a supervisee who sat attentively but rigidly. Her reports of the therapy showed she had integrated what I had said, although therapy sessions were somewhat rigidly confined to following discussions of the previous supervisory session. We seemed to inch forward, her spontaneous participation increasing by the smallest of degrees. I drew attention to the structure of her therapy sessions, her integrations of learning, and made tentative approaches toward direct discussion of our relationship (i.e., She: "I wish I had a map." I: "And I'm not giving you one.") In addition, she began spontaneously to raise questions about her patients' fears in relationships. I found myself inhibited in pursuing either my initial efforts or in asking her directly if she might be speaking of us in the questions she raised. Instead, I asked her to elaborate, in response to which she would brighten. I found her ideas interesting.

Two incidents moved us forward more rapidly, in response to which the therapy also expanded in scope, departing from her need to have it follow closely the scope of the previous supervisory session. One was initiated by her when she began by saying she'd been feeling inadequate in what she knew, and she always felt she had to hide this. This led me to tell her how I had been feeling with her, respectful of her work but uncomfortable with her, shut out, and puzzled. She grew sad and revealed her conflicted wish for a connection with me. We both noted that neither of us had felt connected.

The second incident was in response to a project I had of videotaping an early supervisory session, which we watched several months after this first focal conversation. There was an incident where she glossed over having better anticipated something about the patient than I did. We both also noted our anxiety on tape, which led to her surprise that I had been anxious. This led again to addressing the inscrutable stance she used to protect her from anxiety, and her saying this time that she always felt she had to hide what she knew, that her father liked teaching her things, but seemed hurt or angry when she learned them. After this discussion, she was able to pursue certain themes better with her patient, and her clinical talent increasingly emerged.

Several months later, she said, "Getting things out made a difference. I thought a lot was going on with me, but that you were untouched. I wanted something with you—a connection— but unless I was sure I could have it, I shouldn't want it. When you said you were confused and anxious, it made you more real. I think, without realizing it, I imagined you must be criticizing me. Once we started opening things up, I didn't have to keep guarding against you criticizing me, and that made it easier with my patient, too."

If difficulties in the supervisory relationship are not worked out, they will inevitably appear in some form in the therapeutic relationship (Caligor 1981). A supervisee injured in supervision will act out these injuries with the patient, in confused attempts to repair them. For example, supervisees who feel inadequate in super-vision, particularly with a supervisor who teaches primarily through giving personal perceptions, formulations, and techniques, may then act with their patients as though they have all the answers, thus stifling their patients' self-exploration. If supervisees feel criti-cized by the supervisor, they may try to gain a degree of control by becoming critical of their patients in turn, or they may try to give to the patients in ways to make up for what they feel they do not get, by an overpermissive stance that fails to encourage patients in self-examination.

THE MEDIUM: LANGUAGE

[Our fundamental tool of communication, language, is the medium through which we move toward our goals. While all language is limited, due to its representational nature, the language of psychoanalysis is particularly reductionistic. It is vastly abbreviated relative to the never-ending layered phenomena it describes. Thus, there is a need for ongoing attention to specificity of terms[We come to assume we know exactly what we mean by *working through*, *oedipal conflict*, and *projective identification* until we begin to articulate their meaning]Then we also begin to appreciate how difficult this is and therefore how great a challenge it is for the supervisee to understand our terminology. Related to this is that we often become so intrigued with understanding the patient, we fail to address explicitly what to do with that understanding. In keeping with the appreciation that there are many ways of moving toward a goal, a focus on the process of what questions to raise in making technical decisions is best suited to the work.

It is difficult for those who have little experience as patients to relate to the multitude of phenomena that are unconscious. Although the psychoanalytic language points to what many know intuitively, this knowledge is vague and elusive. Thus, it is a difficult language to teach. At the same time, its students are highly articulate people, so the frustration in understanding it often leads to an increase in self-doubt and perfectionistic strivings, before pleasure can be taken in the process.

[An opportunity for modifying perfectionism through supervision lies inherent within the tool of language.(Both the process of therapy and the teaching of it depend on language)Yet language, only symbolic of experience, can never capture experience in its entirety. At the same time, we remain dependent on it for inter-change. Thus, through our very medium of exchange, we are deal-ing with the inevitability of imperfection and the need to negoti-ate resulting frustrations and disappointments, while maintaining connectedness and positive self-esteem. Words themselves make the supervisory process a developmental opportunity for the re-linquishment of omnipotence in favor of acceptance of realistic possibilities and limitations, of replacing unattainable aspirations with attainable ones. Engaging in a dialogue between two lan-guages, we must somehow create a third, through which we can both discover individual meanings and negotiate shared ones, through which we can come both to understand each other bet-ter and to appreciate that we can never totally understand. Words, applying to general classes of things, are likely to mean one thing to the patient, another to the supervisee, and a third to the supervi-sor. The negotiation of this dilemma is the establishing of a work-ing alliance (Stern 1984).

In supervision, the discovery, negotiation, and revision of meaning not only teaches the treatment process, it enacts a replace-ment of perfection as an ideal with that of ever-evolving comple-tions. The ongoing struggle to move toward a more satisfying ver-bal expression of our thinking involves many complete moments, as ideas are identified and synthesized. At the same time, as new elements are added and contexts change, the definition of comple-tion for the next moment also changes. In a sense, language is al-ways transitional, as in the concrete instances when the supervisee repeats the supervisor's words in the session.

Language as a tool of treatment poses particular difficulties because we deal so heavily with affectual experience, and language is poorly equipped to deal with affectual subtleties. While occasion-ally words or phrases beautifully capture an experience, more often they reflect only fragments of it. In fact, words complicate our task by driving whole segments underground. Thus, language disowns as it helps to own and leads to misunderstanding as it helps to understand (Stern 1985).

Furthermore, we never know how much of what we are trying to deal with rests on preverbal experience. Certain experiences seem to go beyond words and therefore seem unknowable, perhaps because they existed before words. There is a tendency to be critical when something is difficult to articulate, rather than to consider this a problem inherent in the limits of language.

Because we are so dependent on language in both treatment and supervision, we are forced to stick with its challenges. When met, there is a powerful discovery that only each individual can decide what words mean. For supervisees, this augments autonomous functioning and ameliorates pain as they truly experience there is no one "right" answer. The negotiation of shared meanings and misunderstandings strengthens the experience of connectedness as appreciation of its limits develops. All of this is, of course, then brought to the patient. Respect and appreciation grow for the ever-unfolding nature of the patient's story and development.

⌐ As supervisees learn to judge less, adopting a more comfortable position of active-passivity, asking for more details of the patient's experience, following the moment-to-moment shifts within the session, and using their own associations and countertransference, the reporting of the treatment during the supervision changes. The process and the patient leap to life. Pleasure in discovery replaces determination to do it right.⌐

CONCLUSION

Perfectionism as discussed here is so commonplace, one wonders what factors might make so many so vulnerable to it. The self and sense of self develop in part directed to the self (i.e., perception through sensory modalities, feelings, instincts, physiological sensations, memory) and in part directed outward, related to the world, particularly of self with other (Winnicott 1958a, Stern 1985). Then, throughout life, as Winnicott (1958a) has noted, the relating of inner and outer reality constitutes an ongoing strain. Successful integrations of the two are creative experiences, from which the individual gains a sense of continuity and "going on being" (Winnicott 1965). Those that are unsuccessful perhaps arise either from an inadequate consideration of outer reality (leading perhaps to psychosis or psychopathic development) or from an inadequate consideration of internal reality. In these latter cases, where the negotiation of the differences becomes an attempt to adapt primarily to some external need, for example, of a parent, or to some external standard, for example, of society, perhaps perfectionistic strivings ensue. Given that such a need or standard is not internally generated, it may seem never to be met adequately enough, because the contextual organization is impaired through inability to consider adequately all relevant realities.

Winnicott (1958a) conceived of the false self as developing to the extent that the parent is limited in ability to validate the infant's and young child's spontaneous gestures, wanting something else instead. The child then becomes more attuned to the parent's wish than to her own and strives to meet it. Winnicott's formulations rest on limitations in the parent–child relationship during preverbal experience. Through therapy, unfoldings of patient experience in early childhood once language is acquired frequently indicate that many children, in trying to make sense of their disappointment, hurt, and anger, conclude that there is something wrong with them. This might lead them to strive to correct the uncorrectable, or toward perfectionism. Such a resolution might then lead to the striving I noted in the beginning of this chapter, of supervisee striving to know the unknowable, fix the unfixable, and love the unlovable.

In observing young children, one notes the intensity of their passions and the difficulty in accurately understanding their inner worlds, due to their limited language. Adequacy of attunement, so much a matter of degree, is hard to assess. Thus, many may be vulnerable to these kinds of strivings, to the extent that the above thoughts have some validity.

Whatever leads us to choose to be psychotherapists and supervisors, these roles always involve us both in mediation of our own inner and outer realities and in facilitating this in others.

In *Alice in Wonderland,* the caterpillar took the hookah out of his mouth and asked, "Who are you?" "I hardly know, sir, at the present—at least I knew this morning when I woke, but I think I must have changed several times since then," Alice replied. As supervisees have something of this in common with Alice, it is hoped that we can be of help in the fullest sense.

REFERENCES

Allphin, C. (1987). Perplexing or distressing episodes in supervision: how they can help in the teaching and learning of psychotherapy. *Clinical Social Work Journal* 15(3):236–245.

Arlow, J. (1963). The supervisory situation. *Journal of the American Psychoanalytic Association* 11:576–594.

Bergman, A. (1978). From mother to the world outside: the use of space during the separation-individuation phase. In *Between Reality and Fantasy,* ed. S. Grolnick and L. Barkin, pp. 145–165, New York: Jason Aronson.

Brightman, B. (1984). Narcissistic issues in the training experience of the psychotherapist. *International Journal of Psychoanalytic Psychotherapy* 10:293–317.

Bromberg, P. (1982). The supervisory process and parallel process in psychoanalysis. *Contemporary Psychoanalysis* 18:92–121.

Caligor, L. (1981). Parallel and reciprocal processes in psychoanalytic supervision. *Contemporary Psychoanalysis* 17:1–27.

Deri, S. (1978). Transitional phenomena: vicissitudes of symbolization and creativity. In *Between Reality and Fantasy,* ed. S. Grolnick and L. Barkin, pp. 43–60. New York: Jason Aronson.

Doehrman, M. J. G. (1976). Parallel processes in supervision and psychotherapy. *Bulletin of the Menninger Clinic* 40(1):9–20.

Ekstein, R., and Wallerstein, R. S. (1958). *The Teaching and Learning of Psychotherapy*. New York: International Universities Press.

Epstein, L. (1986). Collusive selective inattention to the negative impact of the supervisory interaction. *Contemporary Psychoanalysis* 22(3):389–409.

Fleming, J., and Benedek, T. (1966). *Psychoanalytic Supervision*. New York: Grune & Stratton.

Gediman, H., and Wolkenfeld, F. (1980). The parallelism phenomenon in psychoanalysis and supervision: its reconsideration as a triadic system. *Psychoanalytic Quarterly* 49:234–255.

Goin, M. K., and Kline, F. (1976). Countertransference: a neglected subject in clinical supervision. *American Journal of Psychiatry* 133(1):41–44.

Grinberg, L. (1979). Countertransference and projective counter-identification. *Contemporary Psychoanalysis* 15:226–247.

Kennedy, H., and Yorke, C. (1982). Steps from outer to inner conflict: superego precursors. *Psychoanalytic Study of the Child* 37:221–228. New Haven: Yale University Press.

Kohut, H. (1971). *The Analysis of the Self*. New York: International Universities Press.

Lakovics, M. (1983). Classification of countertransference for utilization in supervision. *American Journal of Psychotherapy* 37(2):245–257.

Loewald, H. (1980). On the therapeutic actions of psychoanalysis. In *Papers on Psychoanalysis*, pp. 221–256. New Haven: Yale University Press.

Lowrer, R. (1972). Countertransference resistances in supervisory situations. *American Journal of Psychotherapy* 129(2):156–160.

Lubin, M. (1984). Another source of danger for psychotherapists: the supervisory introject. *International Journal of Psychoanalytic Psychotherapy* 10:25–45.

Mahler, M., Pine, F., and Bergman, A. (1975). *The Psychological Birth of the Human Infant*. New York: Basic Books.

McDougall, J. (1985). *Theatres of the Mind: Illusion and Truth on the Psychoanalytic Stage.* New York: Basic Books.

Miller, A. (1981). *Prisoners of Childhood.* New York: Basic Books.

Mulsin, H., and Val, E. (1980). Supervision and self-esteem in psychiatric teaching. *American Journal of Psychotherapy* 34:545–555.

Racker, H. (1957). The meanings and uses of countertransference. *Psychoanalytic Quarterly* 26:303–357.

Searles, H. F. (1965a). Problems of psychoanalytic supervision. In *Collected Papers on Schizophrenia and Related Subjects*, pp. 584–604. New York: International Universities Press.

————. (1965b). The informational value of the supervisor's emotional experiences. In *Collected Papers on Schizophrenia and Related Subjects*, pp. 157–176. New York: International Universities Press.

————. (1975). The patient as therapist to his analyst. In *Tactics and Techniques in Psychoanalytic Therapy*, vol. 2, ed. P. Giovacchini, pp. 95–151. New York: Jason Aronson.

Stern, D. (1985). *The Interpersonal World of the Infant.* New York: Basic Books.

Winnicott, D. W. (1958a). Ego distortion in terms of the true and false self. In *Through Paediatrics to Psychoanalysis*, pp. 140–152. New York: Basic Books.

————. (1958b). Transitional objects and transitional phenomena. In *Through Paediatrics to Psychoanalysis*, pp. 229–242. New York: Basic Books

————. (1965). The theory of the parent–infant relationship. In *The Maturational Processes and the Facilitating Environment*, pp. 37–55. New York: International Universites Press.

4

Dealing with the Anxiety of Beginning Therapists in Supervision

SUSAN REIFER

Both beginning therapists and their supervisors have the daunting task of finding the optimal atmosphere to facilitate learning. Supervisors are concerned about the student and his capacities. Will he be supervisable? Will his characterological problems interfere with his ability to learn? These worries of supervisors often dovetail with the worries of beginning students. They too are concerned about their ability to successfully master the difficult process of becoming a therapist. As a result, they often have a great deal of anxiety.

Learning to do therapy is unlike most other kinds of learning. As stated by Brightman (1984), "[T]he instrument of the practice is in large measure the personality of the practitioner itself, with professional success or failure being viewed to some degree as a reflection on the therapist's own character development and functioning" (p. 295). The risks for the student, therefore, seem particularly great, as he worries that his personality will be judged along with his work and, should he be unsuccessful, he is likely to suffer serious narcissistic injury. As a result, the student is likely to approach the learning process with a high degree of ambivalence, which will result in the development of defensive strategies to protect himself from injury.

As early as 1933, Jessie Taft, in an abstract on social work education, commented on the need for the student to recognize the negative feelings about learning that arise during training. Robinson (1949) later expanded on Taft's concerns, discussing the inevitable development of oppositional feelings on the part of supervisees in the supervisory situation. The probability that these oppositional feelings stem from the vulnerability of the student in supervision has also been discussed by Fleming and Benedek (1966), who recognize the student's fear of being found wanting and his worry about failure and the sense of humiliation this will bring. This fear and the defensive maneuvers undertaken by students have been recognized by other authors such as Dewald (1981), who talks about how the psychoanalytic educational process stimulates regressive behavior patterns in students which may take different forms. Arlow (1963) comments on the need for supervisors to understand confusion on the part of students as part of the normal learning experience. The supervisor's worries about the supervisee's performance and its reflection on him (especially when the supervisors are in training programs or being evaluated) can lead the supervisor to disregard the often intense anxiety and the form it takes in supervisees. As a result a learning alliance is not solidly established and the student learns little.

FEELINGS OF OMNIPOTENCE

All the above authors give recognition to the strong feelings often generated in beginning therapists by the process of learning to do therapy. The highly charged emotional factors at work during therapy hours with the patient are compounded by the emotional response the student therapist often has toward the supervisor (Doehrman 1976). The beginning therapist is required to present his work to a stranger whom he must trust will not injure him narcissistically, as he exposes his work and himself. The supervisee is flooded with worry and resistance, both in his relationship to the supervisor and in his struggle to do the therapeutic work. The preoccupation with the possibility of narcissistic injury often leads the beginner to assume the grandiose professional self discussed by Brightman (1984). This grandiose ideal—the all-knowing, all-loving, and all-powerful therapist—is easily shattered (Teitelbaum 1990). The student discovers very quickly that he is not all-knowing. And to the patient, because of the vicissitudes of the transference, he is sometimes seen as a frightening object rather than a loving one. These realizations increase the pressures on the beginning therapists who are often convinced that the grandiose ideals they hold are also held by both supervisors and patients. The awareness of new therapists that their skills do not match those of experienced therapists often contributes measurably to their anxiety with their patients, as well as in supervision. The student therapist has to contend with the failure of the defensive measures he employs to reduce his anxiety about doing therapy, as well as his fear of the judgment of his supervisor, on whom he often projects his own harsh superego demands. In addition, he must contend with the expectations of patients and his own feelings of responsibility for their welfare.

> An example of this is a supervisory session in which a new therapist brought up her concerns about her manic depressive patient's stability. The patient's mother, also a manic depressive, whom she was symbiotically tied to, was developing manic symptoms. The therapist was alarmed as the patient was becoming increasingly agitated and she worried that the mother's symptoms would trigger a manic episode in the patient. She felt it was her responsibility to prevent the patient from becoming psychotic and, toward that end, was encouraging the patient to act as a selfobject for the mother. The supervisee was greatly relieved to discover that her supervisor did not consider it her responsibility to ensure that the patient

did not have a manic episode. In this instance the therapist's anxiety about the patient paralleled the patient's anxiety about her mother. She was convinced that the supervisor would require her to be as omnipotent with the patient as she required of herself, and the patient's mother required of the patient. As she felt inadequate to the task, she asked to borrow some of the supervisor's omnipotence to "save" the patient. When the supervisor made it clear to the student that she did not consider herself omnipotent and had no such expectations for the student, the student was very relieved and was freed from her countertransferential need to save the patient and the patient's mother. In addressing this case, by addressing the supervisee's anxiety about needing to be omnipotent, the supervisor was able to help the supervisee successfully address the parallel process between the mother and patient and the patient and therapist, as well as the therapist and supervisor.

This supervisee's anxiety about her responsibility toward the patient is common in new therapists. Theorists have hypothesized that this is the result of the entrance into the field of those who wish to "master the narcissistic trauma and damage created by being 'used' by the parent as a supporting object at a time in development when these symbiotic roles should be just the reverse" (Brightman 1984, p. 295). In curing the patient, the therapist attempts to move toward repairing the damage done to him as a child. His omniscient need to know and omnipotent need to keep the patient from deteriorating represent his attempts to restore a sense of mastery over a childhood situation in which he felt overwhelmed and unprotected. This need on the part of the new therapist to cure the patient of his symptoms is compounded by the current consumer climate, in which patients often expect the therapist to cure their symptoms as well, without requiring them to become introspective about their genetic roots or characterological issues generally.

In light of the supervisee's worries about being evaluated by the supervisor, his inner psychic pressures and patient demands for quick results, it is no wonder that new therapists are often intensely anxious. This anxiety often results in regression so that the student's strengths may not be readily apparent, while his weaknesses may appear glaring. The student's performance may be a function of the mobilization of primitive defenses or the increased rigidity of existing defenses in the face of anxiety generated by the process of learning to become a therapist. The supervisor's need to make a learning diagnosis is impeded by the amount of anxiety exhibited by the supervisee. The supervisor ultimately has the task of determining whether the supervisee's problems in doing the work are due to serious characterological problems, temporary regression because of his anxiety, or the result of parallel processes in the supervision and treatment.

Many times supervisees are labeled by their supervisors as being rigid, narcissistic, dependent, or concrete, because of the regression which accompanies the beginning of the learning process. In such cases, the supervisor has often not paid enough attention to what Fleming and Benedek (1966) call the learning alliance. They suggest that this alliance is like the working alliance in therapy. The creation of a firm learning alliance is made difficult by the different defensive reactions of students. The supervisor is faced with the task of tailoring different approaches to different students based on their learning needs. Ekstein and Wallerstein (1958) also touch on the need to start where the student is in doing supervision. By doing this the supervisor can create a safe environment for the beginning therapist.

APPROACHES TO REDUCING ANXIETY

Different supervisees may need different approaches to reduce anxiety. Many need an empathic holding environment to feel safe. This often means that didactic considerations take a back seat to helping the student become comfortable doing therapy. This approach can be a stressful one for supervisors, who feel that, ethically, they must not neglect the interests of the patient (Lebovici 1970). Often, despite misgiving, the more empathic approach does not result in the sacrificing of the patient's interests. The decrease in anxiety experienced by the student because he feels supported by the therapist often results in identification with the supervisor and the development of a more empathic approach to the patient, with the result that both patient and therapist are well served.

With other students, anxiety is reduced by a more didactic approach. When the supervisee uses intellectualization heavily as a defense, or when he regresses to a dependent position initially, anxiety may be reduced by receiving information. Although some authors warn against giving too much information to students for fear they will become too dependent (Wagner 1957), other authors recognize the need to be more generous with some supervisees (DeBell 1981). Frequently, as students' anxieties are reduced, they begin to develop both their own style and become more confident in expressing their opinions about what is going on in the process between them and the patient and how to address it. The supervisor can, as the student grows, become less didactic and help the therapist continue to develop his own thinking and style. The supervisor needs to maintain a degree of flexibility and perhaps modify, at least initially, his style to develop a strong learning alliance with the supervisee which will facilitate optimal learning.

In order to remain flexible, the supervisor may need to decide which of the three types of supervisory methods discussed by Wagner (1957, based on his seminars with Ekstein) would be appropriate for his student. Should he take a patient-centered approach, in which "the student brings his technical problems with the patient to the supervisor and is given advice" (p. 760); should he take a therapist-centered approach, in which the focus is on the therapist's countertransference reactions and his blind spots; or should he take a process-centered approach, in which the emphasis is on the interaction between therapist, patient, and supervisor?

The process-centered approach is the one most often followed in supervision. Ekstein and Wallerstein (1957), in discussing this approach, recognize that learning in psychotherapy is both intellectual and emotional and the two must be integrated for the therapist to be successful. This method presumes that the therapist's learning problems with the patient are often paralleled in the student's relationship with the supervisor. However, the beginning therapist's anxiety and inexperience, rather than intrinsic problems in learning, may trigger this parallel process.

Some supervisors prefer a therapist-centered approach which, as Wagner points out, may slide into more of a psychotherapeutic relationship with the student. This approach may escalate the anxiety of the student, if it is not used with sufficient tact and discretion. The student can feel as though he is being analyzed and become more defensive as a result.

Wagner talks about the patient-centered approach as being the most soothing for the beginning therapist who may, at first, feel secure and later feel like a passive puppet of the supervisor.

In fact, as Wagner suggests, all of these approaches are intertwined. In deciding which one to pursue, the supervisor should consider the level of anxiety of the student and how it can best be reduced. How this anxiety manifests itself needs to be noted by the supervisor, who must make a preliminary learning diagnosis of the beginning therapist's defensive coping style. After doing this, the supervisor can better decide which teaching method will provide the safest environment for the student so that he can become more comfortable with the learning process. To produce optimal learning, the supervisor must maintain a flexible teaching style.

REFERENCES

Arlow, J. A. (1963). The supervisory situation. *Journal of the American Psychoanalytic Association* 11:576–594.

Brightman, B. K. (1984). Narcissistic issues in the training experience of the psychotherapist. *International Journal of Psychoanalytic Psychotherapy* 10:293–317.

DeBell, D. E. (1981). Supervisory styles and positions. In *Becoming a Psychoanalyst*, ed. R. Wallerstein, pp. 39–60. New York: International Universities Press.

Dewald, P. A. (1981). Aspects of the supervisory process. *The Annual of Psychoanalysis* 9:75–89.

Doehrman, M. (1976). Parallel processes in supervision and psychotherapy. *Bulletin of the Menninger Clinic* 40:9–20.

Ekstein, R., and Wallerstein, R. S. (1958). *The Teaching and Learning of Psychotherapy*. New York: Basic Books.

Fleming, J., and Benedek, T. (1966). *Psychoanalytic Supervision: A Method of Clinical Teaching*. New York: Grune & Stratton.

Lebovici, S. (1970). Technical remarks on the supervision of psychoanalytic treatment. *International Journal of Psycho-Analysis* 51:385–392.

Robinson, V. (1949). *The Dynamics of Supervision under Functional Controls: A Professional Process in Social Casework*. Philadelphia: University of Pennsylvania Press.

Taft, J. (1933). *Living and Feeling*. New York: Child Study Association of America.

Teitelbaum, S. (1990). Supertransference: the role of the supervisor's blind spots. *Psychoanalytic Psychology* 7:243–258.

Wagner, F. F. (1957). Supervision of psychotherapy. *American Journal of Psychotherapy* 11:759–767.

5

Transference in Analysis and in Supervision

WILMA COHEN LEWIS

It is well known that transference is ubiquitous and that it occurs in all human relationships. The supervisee will experience many of the same transference feelings and distortions so often seen in analysis whether or not the supervisor intends to elicit them or work with them. Intense transference projections and displacements, both positive and negative, are triggered in the supervision process as they are in analysis.

The difference between analysis and supervision, and it is a crucial difference, is that in analysis the transference is encouraged to expand. The conditions of analysis are designed to safeguard the transference and allow it to expand. The ground rules of classical analysis include the fundamental rule of free association; the frequency of sessions; the rule of abstinence; the analyst's neutrality; the analyst as a reflecting mirror; and the need for relative anonymity. The analyst does not reveal too much of himself. The analyst abstains from too much transference gratification (Freud 1912).

The analytic attitude of relative anonymity and relative neutrality perform an essential function in the psychoanalytic process. They provide the keystone for the entire system of abstinence and serve as the chief stimulus for the regression that leads to performance neurosis: the crux of the analytic process, the path to the goal, the means to an end by which the patient's neurosis can be worked out. In treatment, transference is the central vehicle of cure.

In supervision, however, intense transferences can become an obstacle to learning. Here you do not want the transference to expand. You want to nip these nascent issues in the bud. The success of supervision in facilitating learning will depend on the avoidance of intense transferences, particularly the negative transference.

Most supervisees approach supervision with a great deal of anxiety about their performance, about whether they are good enough to do the work. According to Robert Berk (personal communication 1987), this ego–superego conflict is often experienced consciously or preconsciously as "Am I good enough to do this work?" "Can I measure up?" In her anxiety about living up to her ego ideal, the supervisee defensively projects her own punitive superego, her own "bad" critical image, onto the supervisor. It is the supervisor, then, who is expected and perceived to be critical, judgmental, and punitive. I find this particularly true in psychoanalytic training where every candidate is already a fully qualified professional with experience: a fully qualified psychologist, psychiatrist, or social worker. Some are even experts in their field: university faculty members, heads of departments, and contributors to their field. Each now has to be a beginner and a learner of psychoanalysis. Their fear of exposure is great.

[The successful supervisor will be able to allay the anxiety of the supervisee and avoid the development of a negative transference by nipping these issues in the bud (Fielding 1978). Here you are not anonymous or abstinent. Here you are a real person. Here you show your warmth and openness and acceptance. Here you praise, support, encourage, and advise. Here you show empathy to the vulnerability of a learner. Here you share your own experiences, your own mistakes. Here you share your own doubts and anxieties as a learner.)

The unsuccessful supervisor is either not aware of this dynamic or is unable to do this, or both. The supervisee's anxiety continues unabated. The nascent negative transference is exacerbated and becomes an obstacle to learning.

In studying the characteristics of the effective supervisor, Fielding (1978) found that personality traits seemed to be the crucial factor. Of the utmost importance were supervisors who were not judgmental or critical and, therefore, allayed the anxiety of their supervisees. Other important personality traits were: warmth, honesty, good will, understanding, flexibility, respect, concern, empathy, sharing and openness, not theoretical or technical knowledge. Theoretical and technical knowledge were either assumed or considered to be secondary to these other attributes.

It was the supervisor's personality traits that diluted and neutralized the negative superego projections: the tendency of the supervisee to defensively project his own "bad" critical image onto the supervisor. This served to allay the anxiety of the supervisee and to avoid the negative transference so that an optimal situation for learning could be established. The unsuccessful supervisor is unable to do this.

The following are two anecdotes from my own experience as a learner.

EXPERIENCE 1

I began supervision in my first year of analytic training with a supervisor who elicited intense anxiety in me.

I anticipated criticism. I anticipated rejection. I anticipated that he would find me inadequate and wanting.

My supervisor was actually fairly anonymous. He shared some few experiences but never mistakes or messes. He was cool and not particularly open. He would sit silently and watch me as I struggled to find words to express myself. He did not praise, support, or encourage. My anxiety mounted.

When I got up the courage to talk about how anxious I felt with him, he handled it analytically. He asked whether there was anything he had done or said. I said, "No," because I had no insight into what was going on. In my attempt to explore it further, I began to associate to feelings about the chairman of my department in graduate school with whom I did not feel so anxious. He interrupted me and told me to save my associations for my analyst. It was my problem!

My anxiety intensified. My negative superego projections intensified. Now it was no longer criticism that I anticipated. It had been confirmed by him! In the silences that grew longer when I would struggle to express my thoughts, he would sit silently and look at me impassively. At times I was so anxious that I struggled to speak. As far as the learning was concerned, I felt as though I might as well have not been there. It was excruciating.

In retrospect, I now understand that because he maintained a purely analytic stance, my anxiety was heightened and my negative transference expanded.

EXPERIENCE 2

Here is another experience in supervision, with the same components but a very different outcome.

Several years later, I went into private supervision with an analyst who is known and respected for his theoretical knowledge and clinical skills. Transference potential was complicated further because I was already a graduate of his institute.

I knew the supervisor and I knew he thought well of me. Here, I had something more to lose, his good opinion.

My anxiety and defensive negative superego projections were rampant at the beginning of supervision.

But he was warm. He talked. He shared. He was encouraging. He talked to me like a colleague. He praised. He expressed confidence in me. He shared his own experiences with patients, sometimes mistakes. He shared his questions and his doubts. At times he even shared aspects of his own psychodynamics to make a point. He listened, respected me, and was available as a mentor. When I told him at the beginning of supervision that I was anxious and had avoided this supervision for a long time, he shrugged and said, "You have some transference to me." Normal, natural, no big deal. Even this was handled in a nonjudgmental and noncritical way.

He allayed my anxiety and diluted and neutralized my negative superego projections, my tendency to project my own "bad" critical image.

In this supervision, I was open. I was relaxed. I was eager and excited about learning. We tackled clinical questions. We tackled theoretical questions. My clinical work and my own work as a supervisor improved. I did not have nearly enough time for all I wanted to talk about.

I even wondered, "Can you go to supervision twice a week?"

Same psyche. Same potential. Very different outcome.

Transference issues, potential nascent transference projections, and displacements are triggered in supervision as they are in analysis. The way in which the supervisor handles these budding issues, these potentialities, will determine their impact as well as the success of the supervision. Whether intense transference reactions continue, are reinforced, and become obstacles to learning, or are diluted and neutralized will depend upon the personality of the supervisor as well as his conscious or unconscious insight into this dynamic.

REFERENCES

Fielding, B. (1978). The supervisor—facilitating and/or hindering learning in a psychoanalytically oriented training center. *Colloquium* 1(1):34–38.

Freud, S. (1912). Recommendations to physicians practicing psychoanalysis. *Standard Edition* 12:109–120.

6

Stage Fright in the Supervisory Process

JENNIFER LYONS ROBERTS

We work in the dark. We do what we can. We give what we have. Our doubt is our passion and our passion is our task. The rest is the madness of art.

–Henry James

INTRODUCTION

There are many parallels between the art of performing, the art of psychotherapy, and subsequently the art of supervision. In all three endeavors it is not only what you do, but who you are that permeates and enhances the work. Arlow (1963) compares the supervisory situation to artistic creation and analytic psychotherapy and describes the role of supervisor as, "assistant, teacher, and audience" (p. 593). One's ability to use oneself as a "participant-observer" (Sullivan 1953), an active listener, a facilitator of the "potential space" (Winnicott 1971) to form a positive working alliance, or to listen with a "third ear" (Reik 1949) are all components of that undefinable quality which, when combined with good skills, solid theoretical underpinnings, and fine technical ability, results in the magic of art.

Bernstein (1984) writes, "[T]o play the role of a psychotherapist effectively requires at least as much artistry and skill as that involved in a dramatic performance and the utilization of many of the same skills. . . . As every experienced psychotherapist knows, the ability to play a role, a good sense of timing and drama, sensitivity to audience response, an empathic and creative imagination, and stage presence are often required in a well-played therapeutic sequence" (pp. 173–174). The actor Martin Landau described acting as being in a state of knowing and not knowing, of learning the script and then forgetting it in order to be spontaneous and in the moment. Compare this with Reik (1949) who, while likening a beginning analyst to an actor, writes, "The actor should, when he walks out upon the stage, forget what he has studied at the academy. He must brush it off as if it had never been there. If he cannot neglect it now, in the moment of real performance—if he has not gone deep enough that he can afford to neglect it—then his training wasn't good enough" (p. 20).

If psychoanalysis and supervision are both science and art, technique and magic, intellect and soul, then the same skills we use to facilitate play space and creative freedom in our analysands, allowing them to individuate in the presence of another, might be useful when we work with our supervisees. Supervisors must find creative ways to work with a variety of issues that arise during the supervisory process but none seem more crucial to the learning process than learning to work with a supervisee's narcissistic vulnerability and performance anxiety.

PERFORMANCE ANXIETY

The performing aspect of learning to be a psychotherapist can often lead to the equivalent of performance anxiety, or stage fright, as the supervisee presents his work to the supervisor each week for review. In order to understand the specific dynamics involved in the phenomenon of performance anxiety, two articles by Gabbard, an analyst who has worked extensively with performing artists, are useful. In a thorough literature review, Gabbard (1979) makes several key points about the etiology and accompanying developmental experiences that contribute to the anxiety. Gabbard initially asserts that "stage fright," or performance anxiety, is actually a universal experience that all of us who perform, speak, or stand before an audience experience in varying degrees. With reference to both oedipal and preoedipal conflicts Gabbard cites shame, guilt, and separation anxiety as three major factors. Conflicts around exhibitionism, genital inadequacy, and loss of control produce the affect of shame. Conflicts around the aggression of self-display, fear of destruction of one's rivals, and subsequent retaliation produce guilt. The reactivation of the rapprochement crisis, the fear that asserting oneself will result in the withdrawal of love, produces separation anxiety.

Gabbard (1983) also talks of narcissistic issues that contribute to his understanding of stage fright but is quick to point out that not all performers suffer from narcissistic character pathology, "only that residues of universal developmental experiences of a narcissistic nature are revived in the act of performing" (p. 425). He points to a popular saying in theatrical circles, "You are only as good as your last performance," to illustrate the performer's fragile sense of self-worth that has to be established anew each time he performs. This is not unlike the experience of some supervisees whose fragile sense of professional identity fluctuates from session to session. In the ongoing supervisory process, as in work with performers, the supervisor needs to be aware of "concerns around self-esteem regulation, around self-validation from the response of the audience as a mirroring or idealizing object. . . ." (p. 425).

While conducting research interviews with actors for his book entitled *Stage Fright*, Aaron (1986) postulates, "we were in the realm of dreams and fantasies" (p. xvi), and therefore psychoanalysis was the most effective tool for investigating the unconscious mental processes and the intrapsychic dynamics of the anxiety inherent in stage fright. Like Gabbard, Aaron sees the reactivation of childhood conflicts in the act of performing as key to understanding the etiology of performance anxiety. Citing Mahler's (1975) stages of separation and individuation as triggers for anxiety during the rehearsal phase, Aaron follows Freud's psychosexual stages of development to illuminate key anxieties during the performance phase. Some of his examples are as follows:

1. Audience as breast suggests oral phase anxiety due to the fear of the loss of mother; in other words, separation anxiety. Common symptoms of this type of stage fright are nausea, vomiting, and belching, all of which have oral significance.

2. Audience as evaluator of productions speaks to anxiety over loss of love in the anal phase. "I want to get them to love me for what I've produced" is the displaced wish. Anal phase derivatives are found in actors "underplaying" or "overacting," like holding in or letting go. Aaron quotes Gelb (1977) who provides the following example of anal phase anxiety from the actor George C. Scott who feels "disgusted and revolted and hurt and confused," when the audience does not respond. According to Aaron, Scott is responding "not only to the reality of the audience's disapproval and his own intense anger at them; what he also finds disgusting and revolting are his own unconscious fantasies about the mess that he is producing" (p. 95). And one actor, whose opening night stage fright almost paralyzed him, found that it immediately disappeared when a fellow actor told him not to worry about a thing because everything was going to be awful that night, everyone would be making mistakes. The fear of making a mess is also alluded to by the customary use of the French word *merde* to wish fellow actors luck on opening night.

3. Audience as an incestuous love object reflects castration anxiety at the oedipal phase of psychosexual development. Common derivatives include this quote from a male actor cited in Gabbard's (1979) paper, "I just freeze up when I'm out there in front of an audience . . . they'll see I'm small and inadequate . . . they'll find out there's something lesser there . . . that I have nothing to show." And from a female actor, "They'll see a piece of me raw, naked" (p. 387).

Any or all of these anxieties, in derivative form, may be revived during the act of performing. Aaron contends that performance anxiety is not something to be gotten rid of (since his research shows that it never goes away); rather it is a separate artistic problem that the performer must solve along with other problems of artistic performance.

From my experience, unless the issue of performance anxiety in supervisees is managed adequately, it is very difficult to identify any of the other learning issues. However, it is impossible to know exactly how much anxiety the supervisee is experiencing, how intense the transference reactions, or how narcissistically vulnerable the person is. For the supervisee, like the performer, the show must go on, and the defenses used to buoy self-esteem and maintain ego ideals may mask the underlying disequilibrium. It therefore seems advisable that the supervisor create an environment that affords not only a safe forum for learning but also a spontaneous and creative play space in which the supervisee can develop his or her own professional identity and style in the presence of a benign audience.

NARCISSISTIC VULNERABILITY

Many of the writings on supervision focus on alerting the supervisor to the narcissistic vulnerabilities, the superego and ego ideal sensibilities, and the overall anxieties that supervisees may experience in their various stages of learning to become psychotherapists/ analysts. In her paper on narcissistic vulnerability in supervisees, Gill (1999) offers a clear and comprehensive view of three major concepts supervisors should be sensitive to in their work. They are ego ideal conflicts, self-exposure concerns, and narcissistic character defenses. Like Gabbard (1979) who highlights anxiety around self-exposure, Gill adds another dimension to the performance mix when she elegantly captures the essence of the regressive nature of the student role in supervision. She writes: "In meeting with the supervisor on a regular basis, the supervisee inevitably feels that he is exposing himself not only in terms of his professional competence, but also in terms of his basic personality (thoughts and feelings, both conscious and unconscious) . . ." (see Gill, pp. 24–25, this volume). Moreover, the evaluative function inherent in the supervisory process "evokes regressive inducing memories, associations, and fantasies of his personal history as a student vis-à-vis his teachers and a child vis-à-vis his parents . . . (see Gill, p. 25, this volume).

Gill recommends that the supervisor validate and normalize the supervisee's experiences during supervision, always being mindful of the gap between the ideal self and the experienced self that creates anxiety. She emphasizes careful wording when addressing the supervisee's learning issues, as opposed to strengths and weaknesses, and a greater attentiveness to the unconscious feelings the supervisee may experience with his patient. And, I would hasten to add, with the supervisor as well. Since anxiety can truly impede learning, and, as Gill clearly suggests, there is much in the supervisory situation that can produce anxiety, what else can the supervisor do to help dissipate the supervisee's anxiety?

Given the relatively brief nature of each supervisory relationship in many analytic training institutes, and in internships—one year per supervisor, surely it behooves the supervisor to facilitate a positive working alliance, which contains an atmosphere of safety, as quickly as possible. Quite often the supervision has to end just at the time when the supervisor and supervisee are beginning to hit their stride. When it comes to safety there can be no substitute for time in the analytic relationship, but perhaps in the supervisory relationship some principles from a short-term anxiety-regulating therapy model might be useful in establishing as quickly and efficiently as possible a safe and accepting working environment. One example might be this loose adaptation from Vaillant's (1996) "time-conscious" regulating anxiety model of brief therapy. Two key principles that might be useful to bear in mind when beginning supervision, and throughout, are as follows:

Building a Positive Alliance

Much has been written about the supervisory alliance, which may seem passé, but it clearly requires attunement skills and a willingness to stay with the supervisee's needs, rather than asserting one's own agenda. Teitelbaum (1990) talks of the supervisory alliance as, "the development of a partnership between the supervisor and the therapist, free of a disruptive level of anxiety and devoted to the learning and growing of the therapist" (p. 95). Teitelbaum advocates establishing a contract between supervisor and supervisee, "based on mutually agreed-upon expectations" (p. 98). He warns of collusive tendencies between the two parties which encourage, for example, idealization of the supervisor, or a tacit agreement not to challenge each other, and encourages the supervisor to acknowledge his own errors, blind spots, defensiveness, and insensitivities as they arise in the supervisory process.

Diffusing the Transference Rather Than Facilitating a Transference Neurosis

While it is not the supervisor's place to interpret the transference reactions of the supervisee, anxiety-regulating supervisors are active, supportive, and willing to admit their mistakes, all of which help to diffuse tendencies towards more powerful transference reactions. My own experience with a supervisor, early in my training, who utilized the same model of supervision that she used in treatment, confirmed for me that for this supervisee an authoritarian, abstinent, neutral model of supervision only served to promote powerful transferences and heightened anxiety, none of which aided my learning experience (see Lewis, Chapter 5, this volume). In my regressed student role I experienced preoedipal conflicts around shame, anal phase anxiety about making a mess, and oedipal phase anxiety about inadequacy. My supervisor may have assumed I was less narcissistically fragile than I presented, since I put on a good show and covered my anxiety with ingratiating politeness. However, she found out how precarious my self-esteem was when, during a session in which every intervention I made was questioned, I broke down and cried. I could no longer maintain the delicate balance between my ideal self and my experienced self.

As a result of this experience I have become exquisitely sensitive to the possibility that my supervisees may harbor similar vulnerabilities during the beginning phase of their training. I am also aware that throughout one's career as an analyst, no matter how many years of experience one has had, whenever one presents one's work in front of a supervisor, colleague, class of students, or audience of one's peers, there will always be some level of performance anxiety which will have to be managed.

In keeping with the theme of this chapter, I will conclude with the following quote from the late Sir John Gielgud who spent his life performing on the stage. He said, "Acting is half shame, half glory . . . shame at exhibiting yourself, glory at forgetting yourself" (Gussow 2000, p. 1). As supervisors we must be sensitive towards any shame our supervisees may feel when presenting their work to us so that they can forget *themselves* and focus on the business of learning.

REFERENCES

Aaron, S. (1986). *Stage Fright.* Chicago: University of Illinois Press.

Arlow, J. A. (1963). The supervisory situation. *Journal of the American Psychoanalytic Association* 11:576–594.

Bernstein, A. (1984). Psychotherapy as a performing art: the role of therapeutic style. *Modern Psychoanalysis* 9:171–179.

Gabbard, G. O. (1979). Stage fright. *International Journal of Psychoanalysis* 60:383–392.

————. (1983). Further contributions to the understanding of stage fright: narcissistic issues. *Journal of the American Psychoanalytic Association* 31:423–441.

Gelb, B. (1977). Great Scott! *New York Times Magazine,* Jan. 23, pp. 11–12.

Gill, S. (1999). Narcissistic vulnerability in psychoanalytic psychotherapy supervisees: ego ideals, self-exposure and narcissistic character defenses. *International Forum of Psychoanalysis* 8:227–233.

Gussow, M. (2000). Sir John Gielgud, 96, beacon of classical stage. *The New York Times,* May 23, p. 1.

Mahler, M. S., Pine, F., and Bergman, A. (1975). *The Psychological Birth of the Human Infant.* New York: Basic Books.

Reik, T. (1949). *Listening with the Third Ear.* New York: Farrar, Straus.

Sullivan, H. S. (1953). *The Interpersonal Theory of Psychiatry.* New York: Norton.

Teitelbaum, S. (1990). Aspects of the contract in psychotherapy supervision. *Psychoanalysis and Psychotherapy* 8(1):95–98.

Vaillant, L. M. (1997). *Changing Character: Short-Term Anxiety Regulating Psychotherapy for Restructuring Defenses, Affects, and Attachment.* New York: Basic Books.

Winnicott, D. W. (1971). *Playing and Reality.* Middlesex, UK: Penguin.

7

Superego Issues in Supervision

IRIS LEVY

INTRODUCTION

The role of the superego is an essential topic to explore in the discussion of training future analysts. Like all pedagogical hierarchies, psychoanalytic supervision involves not only the dialectics of teaching and learning, but also culminates in an evaluation of the trainee. The very structure of this situation provides fertile ground for the emergence of superego issues. If not properly addressed, these issues may lead to the failure to form a successful supervisory alliance. Yet it is precisely these superego tensions that are often overlooked in the supervisory relationship.

Freud himself, in a famous passage from "Analysis Terminable and Interminable" (1937), seemed to realize that superego issues are inextricably linked to the process of becoming an analyst.

"he [the analyst] has our sincere sympathy in the very exacting demands he has to fulfill in carrying out his activities. It al-

most looks as if analysis were the third of those "impossible"
professions in which one can be sure beforehand of achieving
unsatisfying results. The other two . . . are education and gov-
ernment. Obviously, we cannot demand that the prospective
analyst should be a perfect being before he takes up analysis,
in other words that only persons of such high and rare perfection should enter the profession. [p. 248]

If we take Freud at his word, that psychoanalysis is an almost "impossible profession," then the training of the prospective analyst
may be even more impossible. Freud is clearly warning us that the
ideal of perfectionism for the future analyst, and by implication
the supervisor, is in itself an unattainable standard. How then does
one find a middle ground between the perfectionism demanded
by the superego and the ineluctable fallibility of imperfect human
beings? In other words, how is the impossible profession possible
after all?

To address this question, I will examine superego issues from
the perspective of both the supervisor and beginning supervisee
in psychoanalytic supervision. I will begin with a brief summary of
the origin and functions of the superego; consider how and why
superego issues are prone to develop in supervision; and offer
suggestions for handling this phenomenon. Two case examples will
be provided as illustrations.

ORIGINS AND FUNCTIONS OF THE SUPEREGO

The superego begins to take shape in the preoedipal phases in
reaction to parental prohibitions and demands, especially in the
anal phase around issues of toilet training. At this time, the aim of
the child is to avoid punishment and gain parental approval. The
superego becomes more solidified in the oedipal phase after the
repudiation of the dangerous murderous and incestuous oedipal
wishes and the concomitant identification with the parent of the

same sex. With more or less successful oedipal resolution, the super-ego increasingly becomes an inner structure, and can be thought of as an internalization of the parental superego. However, the severity of the child's superego is not only dependent upon the strictness or leniency of the parental attitude, but also on the intensity of the child's own aggressive wishes. In other words, "the child's own fantasy is always the decisive factor" (Brenner 1982, p. 124).

The functions of the superego are unconscious. Its aim is to avoid intolerable anxiety associated with dangerous childhood wishes and to establish a system of morality involving approval or disapproval of real or fantasized parental prohibitions. While there is some debate about whether there can be a benevolent super-ego, it seems more likely that, as Freud notes: "The superego seems to have made a one-sided choice and to have picked out only the parents' strictness and severity, their prohibitive and punitive function, whereas their loving care seems not to have been taken over and maintained . . . the superego can acquire the same characteristic of relentless severity even if the upbringing had been mild and kindly . . ." (Freud 1933 [1932], p. 62).

There are many situations in adult life that can provoke the emergence of superego issues, especially those which implicitly resemble authoritarian or parental structures. Psychoanalytic supervision is one of these situations.

THE PSYCHOANALYTIC SUPERVISORY SITUATION

Psychoanalytic supervision is a joint venture designed to facilitate the supervisee's growth and development as an analyst. The beginning student comes to supervision with an explicit expectation of learning, and presumably, the supervisor, a teacher of the psychoanalytic process, has something to teach. However, psychoanalytic supervision demands something beyond analysis and other pedagogical situations. It must include both self-awareness, which is the ultimate aim in analysis, as well as receptivity to the material, which is essential to learning. Supervision demands that both of these issues be addressed. The student is asked not only to learn something new, but also to begin to experience herself as an analyzing instrument. From the supervisor's side, she is expected to teach as well as to critically evaluate not only the candidate's work and learning problems, but also her very suitability as an analyst.

Supervision, in essence, is a relationship between a "superior" and "subordinate," perhaps best analogous to that between master/apprentice. The supervisee is attempting to "master" the skill and craft of psychoanalysis with the guidance of the more experienced supervisor. Therefore, inherent to the supervisory situation is a model of dependency on one side, and authority on the other, within the context of an evaluative situation. The hierarchical structure of this arrangement, along with its attendant anxieties, may foster regression and revive conflicts from early childhood in both the supervisee and supervisor. These conflicts may resonate not only with preoedipal issues involving dependency, power, and control, but also with oedipal issues of competition and aggression. All of these issues can and often do set the stage for powerful superego projections to emerge. As Fenichel (1945) notes, "Superego functions may be easily re-projected . . . onto new authority figures . . . (and) . . . this occurs especially when . . . an active mastery of the external world becomes impossible" (p. 107). The proclivity for superego projections will depend upon the interaction between external environmental demands (i.e., the qualities endemic to supervision) and internal demands (i.e., the character and conflicts of the individual supervisor and supervisee).

SUPEREGO ISSUES INVOLVING THE STUDENT

What then are some of the specific characteristics of psychoanalytic supervision that may foster this phenomenon for the beginning student? First, the beginning student is by definition in a "subordinate" position to the more experienced supervisor. As many authors have noted, the student's reliance on the supervisor, along with the inequality of power, may in itself foster regression. A variety of reactions may ensue, including feelings of inadequacy, competition, hostility, or exclusion from the world of "adult" activity. Second, the student is in the difficult position of having to expose herself and her work, and at the same time knows that she will be "judged" by her supervisor. To add to her anxiety, the criteria for evaluation "tends to be subjective and ambiguous in large part because the skills being evaluated are highly complex, intensely personal, and difficult to measure" (Doehrman 1976, p. 10). This evaluation is made doubly complex since the supervisor is never in a position to directly observe the candidate's actual work with her patient. In addition, the fact that it is not only her work, but also the supervisee herself who will be evaluated, adds to the beginner's sense of vulnerability. Third, the teaching and learning of psychoanalysis goes beyond mere didactics, to include the complicated processes involved in the transmission and acquisition of subtle and, at times, elusive analytic skills. This may further exacerbate the supervisee's anxiety and revive old superego demands. Arkowitz notes that since new solutions are often unclear to the beginner, "Unknowns seem to multiply, leading to anxiety, then to an intensification of a wish for definite answers. Old superego dictates of right and wrong rigidify in an attempt to respond to this need" (see Arkowitz, p. 37, this volume). In short, the novice student often begins supervision with a sense of inadequacy, coupled with a fear of exposure and an expectation of being judged. These issues all conspire to rouse in the beginner intense superego concerns that may cause her to have unrealistic expectations of herself, the patient, and the supervisor. Unlike analysis, where intense transference reactions are expected and promoted to further the analysis, in supervision these reactions may interfere in the learning process. Furthermore, in analysis, the candidate can rely on the analyst's neutrality, while in supervision, the student's abilities are evaluated and judged. As Caruth (1990) notes, because of these qualities, unique to psychoanalytic supervision, "supervision at times may become a more threatening experience than the analysis" (p. 185).

The supervisee must then find a solution to manage her often overwhelming anxiety. One of the most typical compromises is a superego projection onto the figure of the supervisor. Berk (personal communication 1993) has pointed out that the new candidate, in the face of heightened anxiety about meeting some imagined standard of perfection, often projects her punitive superego onto the figure of the supervisor. The supervisor is then experienced as critical and punitive (see also Lewis, p. 76, this volume). The most common manifestations of superego projections on the part of the student seem to be either defiance or submission in response to the real or perceived demands of the supervisor. When any of these reactions become too intense, and are resistant to modification, the true educative aims of supervision are thwarted.

If we remember that the superego is involved with seeking approval and avoiding punishment, we can readily see some of the ways in which defenses against superego anxiety may develop in supervision. One of the most common examples involves the presentation of case material. Students often react in one of two extreme ways: either they resist bringing in process recordings or they obsessively transcribe taped sessions. Both are attempts to cope with the anticipation of the supervisor's judgment.

Just as supervisors may become superego figures for the student, beginning students also have a tendency to take the stance of superego figures with their patients. In other words, identification with the aggressor is a common defense used by candidates to ward off superego anxiety. Beginning candidates often make the mistake of either giving or withholding approval to patients. In a related vein, beginners often take credit for "positive" changes in the patient, and blame the patient for movement in a "negative" direction. Students' attempts to become overly supportive or to "rescue" their patients also reveal defensive superego processes. All these stances are compromises designed to diminish superego anxiety via projection of guilt, or defense against aggression, respectively. Thus, one of the most difficult tasks for any supervisor working with a beginner is to help her to develop an analytically neutral stance. Since unresolved superego issues may compromise neutrality, students should be made aware of their tendency to act as superego figures so that they may continue the work of analysis.

SUPEREGO ISSUES INVOLVING THE SUPERVISOR

It has often been noted that raising a child reactivates childhood conflicts in the parent. Likewise, having a novice student may arouse old conflicts and superego anxieties on the part of the supervisor. Thus, all the above-mentioned anxieties of the student may find their counterpart in the supervisor. Some of the most typical superego concerns for the supervisor are anxieties about her teaching abilities, her role as an authority figure, competitive feelings about the student who may one day become her peer or competitor, and the various issues she may have about being in a position of judgment. Finally, the supervisor may have anxiety about being judged herself by the student and training facility.

Obviously, the supervisor's own style, character, and unconscious conflicts will be the determining factor in how she is able to use herself with regard to the unequal power relationship in supervision. The least favorable situation will be one in which the supervisor has profound unresolved superego issues. For example, a competitive and authoritarian supervisor may unconsciously provoke a student to either rebel or comply in a way that is counterproductive to the educative aims of supervision.

I have previously discussed the student's difficulties in establishing analytic neutrality. I would now like to approach this problem from the supervisor's side. It is frequently the case that an analytic supervisor will become excessively angry or frustrated with a resistant student more than with a resistant patient. Why is it more difficult to maintain neutrality as a supervisor than as an analyst?

Perhaps Issacharoff's (1982) emphasis on the difference between the interpretive function of the analyst and that of the supervisor may be helpful here. In our role as analysts we have the data and authority to make a "complete interpretation," one linking the transference, genetic material, and the contemporary situation. This is not possible or even desirable in supervision. Simply pointing out the student's limitations or learning problems does not have the same dynamic force as an analytic interpretation. A supervisor may often feel that a supervisory stalemate might be more easily resolved if she could simply make a complete interpretation. Most supervisors will try not to traverse this boundary. However a supervisor who feels frustrated by this injunction against analyzing the student may instead inappropriately adopt a punitive stance.

Bromberg (1982) emphasizes another factor that makes it more difficult for the supervisor than the analyst to maintain neutrality. He points out that inherent in the supervisory role is the necessity of "responding to crises, stalemates, impasses and problems," and further that the supervisor's role in fact "permits direct advice-giving and management" (p. 102).

In addition, as many authors have noted, the supervisor is far less likely than the analyst to examine her countertransferential feelings with a student than with a patient. This may be related, in part, to the fact that as supervisors we do not strive to maintain the same "evenly hovering attention" that we do as analysts since our task is more active and goal directed than it is in analysis. Consequently, we are less likely to tune into our own unconscious processes during supervision, and this again may compromise our neutrality.

Finally, the supervisor is always in a position to evaluate the student. Unlike the analyst, she makes "real" judgments about the student's abilities and progress. Whether this takes the form of a sadistic attack or overly positive, uncritical feedback depends, in part, on how conflicted she is in regard to her judging function. However, if the supervisor has more or less resolved many of her own superego issues, the evaluation has the potential to become a valuable tool to further the student's development.

Analytic supervisors must learn to adopt a neutral stance without abnegating their responsibilities as educators and evaluators. This places them in the difficult position of needing to be neutral and non-neutral at the same time. How then are we able to critically evaluate a student's work without becoming a punitive superego figure so that optimal learning may take place?

SUGGESTIONS FOR DEALING WITH SUPEREGO ISSUES IN SUPERVISION

In our role as supervisors, we begin from the standpoint of exposing the novice student to various ways of psychoanalytic thinking and listening so that we may deepen her theoretical knowledge, technical skills, and use of her analytic self. At the same time, the student also requires our feedback. How can we best accomplish this dual task of teaching and evaluation without provoking unnecessary superego reactions?

I would suggest that some tentative strategies for dealing with this problem might be found by applying to psychoanalytic supervision some of the "rules" for conducting an analysis. First and foremost is the establishment of a learning alliance, an analog to the therapeutic or working alliance, as discussed by Zetzel (1956) and Greenson (1967) and considered crucial for the success or failure of a psychoanalytic treatment. Many authors have also stressed the necessity of forming a similar alliance in analytic supervision so that true learning may proceed in an atmosphere of emotional safety. Thus, the supervisor must address herself not only to the student's didactic needs, but also to issues involving her self-esteem. As Teitelbaum (1990) has urged, "the supervisor needs to be sensitive to the supervisees' narcissistic vulnerabilities and attuned to . . . creating a supervisory atmosphere that supports, encourages, and nurtures this aspect of development . . ." (p. 4). In addition, the supervisor must find something to genuinely value and respect in each student. No matter how imperfect the fit between supervisor and student, if the supervisor cannot appreciate some of the student's unique qualities, the learning alliance will remain precarious.

Closely allied to the forming of a supervisory alliance is the establishment of what I would like to call "supervisory neutrality." In analysis, neutrality is defined as "the analyst (taking) a neutral position with regard to the patient's conflicts, not an absence of feeling . . ." (Fine 1990, p. 30). If we apply this definition to supervision, then supervisory neutrality means taking a "neutral" position in regard to the student's learning problems or characterological issues—not a lack of feeling or interest about these problems.

In addition, an assessment of the student's anxiety level and other characteristic defenses will provide a guide to the timing, tact, and dosage of our supervisory interventions. Thus, while we provide the student with critical feedback to sharpen her analytic skills, we take care not to make her feel diminished by her mistakes, both technically and countertransferentially. At the very least, we should begin from the standpoint that the student has the capacity to improve.

In addition, the analytic supervisor can counter the spiraling of unproductive superego projections by giving the student permission to verbalize her dissatisfaction and disagreement with the supervisor. Exploration of these concerns may not only resolve a supervisory stalemate, but may also have the additional benefit of demonstrating to the student that debate and dissent are not punishable offenses, but are crucial to the collaborative effort involved in supervision.

Finally, supervisors can help modify punitive superego demands by showing their students that they themselves are not perfect beings with infallible judgment. Arkowitz suggests that we demonstrate to the student our own "willingness to be imperfect," which includes acknowledging our mistakes and confusion and a capacity to tolerate not only the "limits of what we can give . . . [but also] . . . the ambiguities in both the therapy and supervisory situations" (see Arkowitz, p. 45, this volume). In addition, I would say that we should encourage our students to trust their own perceptions, and when appropriate, defer to their best judgment. This, along with respect for the student's individual style, may provide her with some measure of control in an otherwise unequal relationship.

Brightman (1984) emphasizes that true modification of the professional ego ideal means that the trainee must "mourn the loss of the grandiose professional self" which will then hopefully give way to the "establishment of a new, less perfectionistic ego ideal" (p. 307). This is essentially the same point that Freud made in 1937, as cited above. I would add that the supervisor too must relinquish her own unrealistic expectations of herself and the supervisee. Self-reflection, insight, and if necessary, further analysis can help the supervisor become more alert to the manifestations of the neurotically cruel components of her own superego conflicts.

If some of these attempts at superego modification are successfully achieved on the part of the supervisor, then she will be in a better position to help modulate the supervisee's unrealistic strivings for perfection. Both may then be freer to pursue the true goals of teaching and learning.

What follows are two brief supervisory vignettes, both of which illustrate different superego issues that emerged in supervision with beginning supervisees.

CASE EXAMPLE

M. was a bright, but cold and defensive young woman who adopted a punitive and controlling stance with both me and her patients. When two of her patients threatened to quit treatment, she seemed unconcerned, and insisted, "It's their loss." M. seemed to be equally impervious to the supervision. She dismissed any supervisory comments or teaching points I made and seemed to feel that she was the authority who knew best. Since we were clearly in the grip of a supervisory stalemate, I decided to ask her about her feelings about working with me. M. exploded in an angry tirade. She felt that I was imposing my vision of treatment upon her, and my questions in supervision were designed to trap her. Consequently, she explained that she felt inhibited in sessions with patients because she found herself thinking about what I would have wanted her to say or do. Despite my awareness of the supervisory stalemate, I was unprepared for the affective intensity of her reaction. Upon reflection, I began to understand her response in terms of a projection of her own harsh superego onto me. Fearing punishment, she attacked first. At the same time, I also began to explore my own, perhaps overly demanding standards in supervision, which may have increased M.'s need to employ defenses against her guilt and narcissistic vulnerabilities, with both her patients and me.

Although M. subsequently revealed other issues she had about feeling judged, I refrained from making analytic interpretations, and confined our exploration to the realm of supervision. I tried to redefine our common goal of facilitating her learning, and we began to investigate ways in which this might best be accomplished. We both agreed that she needed to develop a greater receptivity to what was being taught, but that this was quite different from a demand that she accept or agree with every one of my supervisory suggestions. At the same time, I recognized that it was essential to respect her individual style and voice.

In retrospect, I believe that the single most important strategy for working through this stalemate was in my not counterattacking the student (i.e., not behaving as a retaliatory superego figure), but, instead, my exploring the various superego tensions as they unfolded. In addition, it was important to demonstrate to M. that although we might disagree, we could still work together in a collaborative effort. We had intermittent discussions throughout supervision in regard to the above issues, and gradually, M. became increasingly able to trust me, expose her work, and form better alliances with her patients.

CASE EXAMPLE

K. was also a beginning supervisee, but unlike M., she was a natural at psychoanalytic work. K. was bright, warm, and psychologically minded. She developed good working alliances with all of her patients. K.'s superego problem was that she was inordinately self-doubting and self-critical. She berated herself for her "mistakes," and seemed timid about relying on her own perceptions. Likewise, she seemed to look toward me as the omniscient authority with all the answers. These traits made K. overly cautious in the use of herself in sessions, and colluding with her patients to avoid the analysis of difficult issues. Furthermore, her anxiety and obsessive attention to detail sometimes clouded her judgment. For example, her elaborately transcribed notes of taped patient sessions often resulted in her losing the forest for the trees.

K.'s self-critical and somewhat perfectionistic stance was an attempt to cope with her own demanding superego, as well as a way to ward off negative criticism from me, or the emergence of negative transference with her patients. Here again, it seemed necessary to reflect upon and work through some of the salient superego issues.

I began by encouraging K. to rely on her own excellent abilities to formulate hypotheses about her cases. Therapists' "mistakes" and negative transferences were framed as inevitable, indeed, useful parts of the learning and treatment processes. In addition, I attempted to show her that I did not always have all the answers, and that sometimes we needed to muddle through things together. We also experimented with her bringing in less detailed process notes in order to give her an opportunity to more freely discuss the overall dynamics of her cases.

With the gradual decrease in superego anxiety, K.'s work in both treatment and supervision deepened. As she became less fearful of the negative transference, she was able to move from a primarily supportive role to a more analytic one. Likewise, in supervision, she began to feel freer to test out her own ideas, and also became more vocal about her learning needs.

In short, K. gradually became less perfectionistic, and at the same time, was able to take herself more seriously as a professional with a better ability to trust and utilize her unique talents.

Although both of these examples illustrate superego projections, from my perspective as supervisor, I felt much more comfortable in supervising K. than M. K. was not critical or attacking, and did not challenge my authority. The apparent smoothness with which the supervision proceeded initially made it more difficult to discern K.'s learning problems, but also probably enabled me to provide a more facilitating role with her. On the other hand, since I began by feeling more challenged by M., it is likely that I initially adopted a more critical and demanding stance with her.

In retrospect, I realized that my response to each student had to do, at least in part, with some of my own unresolved superego issues involving self-doubts, and unrealistic strivings to be the "perfect" supervisor with the "perfect" supervisee. The more I became aware of these issues, and maintained a nonjudgmental attitude toward the student and myself, the more the supervisory alliance was enhanced.

CONCLUSION

It is the supervisor's special responsibility to become alert to the unresolved superego conflicts in herself and in her supervisee, precisely because of their potentially disruptive influence on supervision. If the supervisor can successfully navigate through the various manifestations of mutual superego projections, she will then have a much better chance of sustaining a successful supervision. She will also be in a better position to distinguish between the overly compliant student, the neurotically oppositional student, and the student who is able to receive, yet question supervision on the road to developing his own style as an analyst. The student may then be more likely to emerge as neither clone nor adversary of the supervisor, but as a participant in the learning process: she will be able to carve out her own authentic professional identity. If some of these goals can be even partially realized, then perhaps the "impossible" profession will become somewhat more possible after all.

REFERENCES

Arkowitz, S. (1990) Perfectionism in the supervisee. *Psychoanalysis and Psychotherapy* 8:51–67.

Brenner, C. (1982). *The Mind in Conflict.* New York: International Universities Press.

Brightman, B. (1984). Narcissistic issues in the training and experience of the psychotherapist. *International Journal of Psychoanalytic Psychotherapy* 10:293–317.

Bromberg, P. (1982). The supervisory process and parallel process in psychoanalysis. *Contemporary Psychoanalysis* 18:92–111.

Caruth, E. (1990). Interpersonal and intrapsychic complexities and vulnerabilities in the psychoanalytic supervisory process. In *Psychoanalytic Approaches to Supervision*, ed. R. Lane, pp. 181–193. New York: Brunner/Mazel.

Doehrman, M. (1976). Parallel processes in supervision and psychotherapy. *Bulletin of the Menninger Clinic*, 41:9–104.

Fenichel, O. (1945). *The Psychoanalytic Theory of Neurosis.* New York: Norton.

Fine, R. (1990). Supervision and the analytic superego. In *Psychoanalytic Approaches to Supervision*, ed. R. Lane, pp. 29–33. New York: Brunner/Mazel.

Freud, S. (1933[1932]). New introductory lectures on psychoanalysis. *Standard Edition* 22:57–80.

———. (1937). Analysis terminable and interminable. *Standard Edition* 23:211–253.

Greenson, R. (1967). *The Technique and Practice of Psychoanalysis.* Madison, CT: International Universities Press.

Issacharoff, A. (1984). Countertransference in supervision: therapeutic consequences for the supervisor. In *Clinical Perspectives on the Supervision of Psychoanalysis and Psychotherapy*, ed. J. Caligor, et al., pp. 89–105. New York: Plenum.

Teitelbaum, S. (1990). The impact of psychoanalytic supervision on the development of professional identity: introduction. *Psychoanalysis and Psychotherapy* 8(1):3–4.

Zetzel, E. R. (1956). Current concepts of transference. *International Journal of Psycho-Analysis* 37:369–376.

8

Supervision as a Selfobject Experience

CAROL MARTINO

A central theme in supervising the analyst-in-training is how to respond to the learning needs of the student while preserving the self-esteem and attending to disorganizing affects (fragmentation anxiety), which sometimes accompanies such learning. Many authors (Brightman 1984, Epstein 1986, Fosshage 1997, Jacobs et al. 1995, Rock 1997, and Teitelbaum 1998), have suggested that creating an optimal learning environment requires attunement to the responsiveness of the supervisee regarding the supervisor's teaching points, listening stance, theory, and personal style. This paper will address the supervisory dyad as a selfobject experience for the beginning therapist-in-training.

ORIGINS AND FUNCTIONS OF SELF-SELFOBJECT EXPERIENCES

Conceived by Kohut (1971), the selfobject is thought of mainly from the point of view of a self-sustaining experience. In other words, it is not the object or person providing the experience, but instead, it is the function that the object or person provides that creates the selfobject experience. Wolf (1988) describes the self-sustaining function of empathy and its centrality in providing a selfobject experience:

> A person's sense of self is enhanced by the knowledge that another person understands his inner experience—that is, is aware of that inner experience and is responding to it with warmly colored positive affects. This phenomenon can easily be observed by paying close attention to one's inner state intro-spectively or by empathically getting in touch with another's inner experience. [p. 36]

Lichtenberg (1983) describes selfobject as:

> aspects of care-givers—mother, father, teachers, etc.—who are experienced as providing something necessary for the mainte-nance of a stable, positively toned sense of self. The mother of an 18 month old, who, at about the same time as the child, rec-ognizes his hunger, functions as a selfobject (close to self as an empathic perceiver of his needs, close to an object in her pro-viding of food). [p. 166]

There are two main types of selfobject experiences out of which the self emerges, the mirroring experience and the idealiz-ing experience. Kohut (1978) conceptualized this emerging self as having a bipolar structure. The experience was organized into two structural locations, depending on their mirroring or idealiz-ing characters. The mirroring and idealizing selfobject experience represent the two poles, the former, ambition and the latter, val-ues and ideals. There is said to be an intermediate area between these two poles that has been described as a "tension arc," which stretches between and harbors the existence of inborn talents and acquired skills (Wolf 1988).

Later Kohut (1984) made significant revisions, presenting a more unified theory of a selfobject unit:

> In view of the fact that we now conceive of the self as consisting of three major constituents (the pole of ambitions, the pole of ideals, and the intermediate area of talent and skills) . . . we subdivide the selfobject transferences into three groups: (1) those in which the damaged pole of ambitions attempts to elicit the confirming-approving responses of the selfobject (mirror transference); (2) those in which the damaged pole of ideals searches for a selfobject that will accept its idealization (idealizing transference); and (3) those of which the damaged intermediate area of talents and skills seeks a selfobject that will make itself available for the reassuring experience of essential alikeness (twinship or alter-ego transference). [pp. 192–193]

Wolf (1994) pointed out that we need to investigate the special selfobject needs that accompany specific life tasks. The developmental line of selfobject relations represents one way to conceptualize the changing necessities for selfobject experiences. Additionally, there are three selfobject experiences that Wolf (1994) describes that illustrate the point of the needed selfobject experiences that characterize the developmental line of the analyst-in-training in relation to the supervisor:

> Adversarial selfobject experiences: a need to experience the selfobject as a benignly opposing other who continues to be supportive and responsive while allowing or even encouraging the self to be in active opposition and thus confirming an at least partial sense of autonomy; the need for the availability of a selfobject experience of assertive and adversarial confrontation vis-à-vis the selfobject without the loss of self-sustaining responsiveness from that selfobject.
>
>   Efficacy experiences: From the awareness of having an initiating and causal role in bringing about states of needed responsiveness from others, the child [student] acquires an

experience of efficacy that becomes an essential aspect of the cohesive self experience.

Vitalizing selfobject experiences: The child [student] needs to have the vitalizing experience that the caregiver [supervisor] is affectively attuned to the dynamic shifts or patterned changes in its inner state. That is, across the specific categories of affect to the crescendos and decrescendos, to the surges and fades of the intensity, timing, and shape of its experiences. [pp. 73–74]

THE SUPERVISORY SITUATION

Let us now consider the supervisory situation, the empathic failures on the part of the supervisor, the selfobject need of the supervisee, and the possible opportunity for building and/or restoring the student's professional self. Wolf (1995) wrote on this topic:

All learning . . . can be seen as the acquisition or rearrangement of some psychological structure . . . we can conceptualize the formation or rearrangement of psychological structure as a process that has been designated the "disruption-restoration sequence" . . . in essence this sequence proceeds as follows during therapy: (1) an accepting and understanding ambiance together with interpretation of defenses allows the mobilization of repressed selfobject needs in the transference; (2) the resulting therapeutic alliance is disturbed with fragmenting disorganization of the patient's self when the patient experiences the analyst as ill-attuned . . . (3) by communicating to the patient his recognition, acceptance, and understanding of the patient's fragmented state the analyst restores the selfobject bond between them; and (4) restoration of the selfobject bond facilitates the reemergence of the self in a cohesive state, which comes together in a rearranged form that reflects the analyst's empathic attunement, having integrated into its structure the new experience with the analyst. . . . [pp. 263–264]

If we apply this concept of the disruption-restoration sequence to the supervisory dialogue, it is easy to see that even though the goal of training the student therapist does not necessitate our affecting the deep structures of the personality (as in psychoanalysis), but the surface level of cognitive capacities and problems about learning, it still often requires from the supervisor the ability to heal the disruption (Wolf 1995).

CASE VIGNETTES

My supervisee, an intelligent and articulate student, had described to me that a focus of his learning was the need to develop an analytic listening stance in order for him to hear the latent content as it emerged from the patient. His tendency prior to this session had consistently been to present from the manifest content, and he was stuck there until we learned to co-participate and expand on how to deepen our understanding of both the patient's experience and the supervisee's experience of the patient.

During this supervisory encounter the supervisee presented me with a session whereby the patient's response to the therapist indicated that a narcissistic injury had occurred during one of their interactions. The patient's experience of this interaction had a relational meaning that was an example of what we had collectively (the patient, the supervisee, and I) decided was a repetitive problematic relational theme in the patient's life. I spontaneously commented on it, intervening too early, it seemed. The supervisee's response was an indication that he had experienced my comment as an interruption to the flow of his presentation. He became rigidly defensive and pushed forward to his point which was quite different than previous understandings he had shared with me about this patient. When I tried to get a further understanding of the disparity between this new understanding and the one that had been previously established, my supervisee appeared to withdraw and was unable to articulate his new understanding.

We had come to an impasse from which neither of us could extricate ourselves, a little confused but powerfully caught in something that I tried to understand from a parallel process perspective. After my feeble attempt at having us both acknowledge our parts in a possible enactment of the core dynamics of the patient being discussed, it still seemed as though something much more real and immediate had taken place between us that had not been attended to. I reconsidered the moments just prior to his presenting this particular session and recalled his look of pride and his opening comments about the fact that the patient had cried in a session for the first time with him. Clearly the supervisee's need at that moment was not to have me follow along as in the usual process of a session, but instead was to have me provide a mirroring selfobject experience. I had failed him in that I did not allow him to present a piece of what was "good work" in its entirety, without interruption, and then to be appropriately commended for it. Upon reflection I then said to him, "I think I missed the boat here in terms of what it was that you were looking for from me today. You really felt a sense of accomplishment with this patient because of the amount of affect that had emerged during this session. I think that you wanted me to be a witness to your good work, and I came in too soon with what I thought the patient meant. You needed me to allow you to present the session in full as it unfolded to the place where you felt you had facilitated a breakthrough with her." I observed that his rather rigid posture had softened quite a bit and he replied, "I'm really glad you said that. I was also aware that we were derailed and wasn't quite sure what I was feeling until now." Fortunately the subsequent sessions had an openness to them that seemed to indicate that we in fact had restored enough confidence in our teamwork to get back on track.

In this example of an early stage in training, a mirroring selfobject experience was needed in order for the supervisee to take in what was necessary to build a sense of efficacy. The restoration by the supervisor of the disrupted supervisory experience, through empathic understanding and explanation, can also model for the developing therapist a way of responding to the mirroring self-object need of the patient.

In another example, a supervisee presented a case in which a young man had entered treatment with the expectation that the therapy would support his ability to better compete at a higher level in his doctoral program. He had struggled unsuccessfully with a debilitating anxiety that had on occasion resulted in his having to take to his bed for a couple of days. The patient had a critical father who had a Ph.D. and was very accomplished in his field, and an absent mother who had, in the first few years of the patient's life, been very occupied with finishing law school. Both parents regularly emphasized the importance of academic achievement, the patient recounting on several occasions that his father said, "You are what you achieve."

The patient also described a lack of emotional support and connectedness with his parents as a result of their preoccupation with their professional lives. They would often miss the cues the small child was sending about his need for empathic attunement and affective responsiveness. The chronic failure on their part to provide a soothing selfobject experience left the child with very few self-soothing mechanisms to fall back on, and he could only function well in relation to his parents when he could prove himself to be like or equal to them in their intellectual capacity and achievement. This archaic selfobject tie to them had been the only way of relating the patient could count on, and so the transference took on a highly intellectualized, debate-like quality, whereby the patient, without affect, would dominate each session by recounting philosophical notions and current academic achievements. These achievements for him were self-sustaining experiences in that while he was doing well they mirrored for him a sense of self. If he failed to come up to the internalized idealized parental standard, his failures would then take him back to a regressive fragmented state and a loss of a core cohesive self.

My supervisee was a bright and articulate person, who at the time was finishing his requirements for his Ph.D. He had an emerging transference to his patient as someone whom he became especially enthusiastic about as a possible candidate for analysis, and he chose to focus on his higher functioning characteristics. He would often present sessions with an admiration for the patient's intellectual capacities, and he explored with him those dynamics that would fit what he viewed as his oedipal strivings and conflicts.

The supervisee focused on transference interpretations based on conflict theory, mistaking the pre-structural developmental deficits as oedipal conflicts. The transference interpretations created a distancing effect in the relationship between therapist and patient, and the patient could only respond to the therapist with superficial compliance. When the patient began to report the reoccurrence of panic episodes and exhibit other symptoms of fragmentation, I thought about introducing the notion of a parallel process as a way of discussing a reconsideration of his approach to the case. My concern was that the therapy had entered into an intersubjective realm of experience whereby the therapist was caught in an enactment of the "parental expectation." Now the patient was stirring up in my supervisee an expectation that he could be a "star" patient who could provide an opportunity to learn about analysis from a classical perspective. The supervisee expanded more and more on a higher level of development than what I felt was beneficial for the patient.

The patient was struggling with a pre-structural developmental deficit. This required supporting his need to begin to self-articulate, and to gain a comfort around self-definition in terms of who he was and what he wanted, apart from the opinions and desires of his parents. The patient was struggling with issues that I would describe as selfobject needs versus autonomy (Wolf 1980). If he could gain the interest of his parents by accomplishing what they needed from him, he could maintain the archaic selfobject tie. As a result, the relationship between them was precariously balanced. Along with his inability to hang on to a cohesive self-system, he struggled with finding his own developing identity apart from them, and he was always fearful of re-creating their lack of responsiveness and reexperiencing the traumatic failure.

Parallel to the empathic failure on the part of my supervisee to recognize this with his patient was my own empathic failure in relation to the supervisee. I, too, failed to consider what Lichtenberg and colleagues (1992) would describe as the selfobject need and motivational priority of the moment (motivation as it relates to self-cohesion and the pursuit of selfobject experiences that eventuate in the shaping of a sense of self). In fact, the teaching point that I was making about the case was the very same matter that had caused a failed selfobject experience for my supervisee. The following illustrates this moment.

In one of our sessions, my supervisee was describing his role in what I felt was an enactment of the parental expectation of the patient. The overstimulation of the patient's grandiose self would eventuate in his feeling overburdened, and he would experience painful tension and anxiety around his parents' grandiose and idealizing expectations. My supervisee unknowingly re-created overstimulation in the therapy by being overly enthusiastic and supportive of the patient's accomplishments, including setting up some of his own goals for the patient, such as increasing the frequency of his sessions. As a result, the patient showed increasing symptoms of fragmentation anxiety which were followed by missed sessions.

After an attempt to invite the therapist to reflect fully on his total range of experience of the patient, as to what was occurring in the therapy, it appeared that the therapist was overlooking the amount of anxiety that was occurring in the patient. It was at this time, during our supervision, that I decided to share some of my observations with him about what I thought was a blind spot in the treatment. The therapist had difficulty recognizing that the patient's grandiosity about his ambitions was a defense against the patient's fragile self—a self that never had the opportunity to explore his unique self-experience around phase-appropriate ambitions and skills, or to appropriately integrate the feeling states which accompany these strivings.

After hearing my understanding of the case, my supervisee quickly and firmly responded by saying, "Well, that's your opinion." To which I then said, "Developmental theory is not my opinion." I later thought about my frustrations and contribution to this impasse and my need to have my supervisee take in an understanding that was quite discrepant from his own. In the subsequent session I explored with him the experience of the previous session. He described feeling force fed by me and he revealed that he had experienced a level of anxiety that impeded his ability to hold on to his way of organizing his understanding of the case.

After acknowledging my failure and then supplying a much-needed mirroring selfobject experience, he was able to reconstitute and further explore his points about the priority he had given to the oedipal strivings of the patient. In addition to the mirroring selfobject experience, there was another type of selfobject experience that was needed by the supervisee. For the first time he was exhibiting with me the importance of an adversarial selfobject experience (Wolf 1994), which I had failed to recognize in the process of the moment.

In the very same way the patient was struggling with his selfobject needs versus his autonomy, so too was my supervisee. His need was to experience a developing professional self in opposition to me, and thus to confirm a partial sense of autonomy without risking the loss of any self-sustaining responsiveness from me. My getting overly caught up in the content of the session caused a missattunement to the kind of selfobject experience my supervisee needed. This created an empathic failure around, first and foremost, the mirroring selfobject experience, followed by the needed adversarial selfobject experience. And, subsequently, this prevented both an efficacy experience and vitalizing selfobject experience (Wolf 1994). I had failed to recognize that the acquisition of skill was secondary. More important was the provision of a selfobject experience that would function to maintain the structure and cohesion of his developing professional self.

In order for my supervisee to take in new or discrepant information, I had to assess, in order of his priorities, what his needs were regarding these selfobject experiences. Having then realized my failures, I returned to the primary position of providing the essential ingredient of a mirroring selfobject experience through a close subject-centered listening of his experience of the patient (Fosshage 1997). We restored and furthered the development of a learning environment with enough safety for him to reestablish his position in the adversarial selfobject experience. He had regained a sense of competence and, subsequently, a feeling of efficacy about his work. This created for him a vitalizing selfobject experience as a result of my affective attunement to the dynamic shifts that had taken place between us, restoring his sense of equilibrium and the supervisory relationship.

AFFECTS, SELFOBJECTS, AND THE SUPERVISORY SITUATION

The task of supervising the analyst-in-training very often involves assisting the supervisee with identifying, differentiating, containing, and synthesizing his emotional experience of the patient. It is important that affect integration occur for the supervisee because of its vital contribution to the structuralization of the student's development as an analyst who is capable of organizing his experience of the patient. Stolorow and colleagues (1987) focus on affect integration and the important implications it has on understanding the curative action of selfobject transferences. They contend that "selfobject functions pertain fundamentally to the integration of affect into the developing organization of self-experience" (p. 66).

In this example of a supervisory case I will focus on the intersubjective role of the supervisory relationship and its challenges in providing a selfobject experience when affect integration does not occur for the supervisee, bringing into view the specific inter-play that can either facilitate or obstruct the process of learning for the analyst-in-training.

CASE VIGNETTE

A supervisee described an overall difficulty in presenting cases in supervision and had, at times, preferred to turn supervisory sessions into an ancillary therapy rather than experience the intense anxiety and discomfort of exposing his work. This difficulty manifested in his inability to be prepared to present process notes, attend supervisory sessions on time, remember or recall salient points of his sessions with his patients, and an overall reluctance to allow any process of the supervision to take place. While exploring this difficulty he explained that the evaluative aspect of the supervision created tremendous anxiety for him. He described a repetitive problematic relational theme involving a critical mother who was an academic. What became clearer to me was his own apparent early childhood experience of chronic selfobject failure by his caregivers. This resulted in a self-structure that had been compromised, particularly around the integration of affect. This in turn contributed to his inability to hold on to a picture of the patient that otherwise might have assisted us in illuminating and informing us about the selfobject needs of the patient.

His presentations of session material were quite sparse, vague, fragmented, and lacking in any real formulations about his experience of the patient. His unorganized way of presenting case material would leave me feeling confused and I would ask clarifying questions in an attempt to get a picture of the patient. Any attempt on my part to gain more information about the patient would create fragmentation anxiety to the point that he could not recall those passages or segments of the session where the patient appeared to be moving toward experiencing affect. The supervisee's reluctance to move in closer was in fact a protective measure to stabilize himself against the overwhelming flood of anxiety he felt while sitting with his patient's affect. The amount of disavowal that would occur would then translate into a description of the patient that was analogous to viewing pieces of a puzzle without the puzzle board or frame in which to arrange them. My own experience of feeling disorganized meant that I could no longer count on a way to order my experience of what was actually occurring in the treatment between my supervisee and the patient, and was confronted with having to suspend my own selfobject need to feel useful as a supervisor.

After accepting my own disorganization as part of the evolving intersubjective context of our meetings, I was then able to overcome my increasing uneasiness and enter into an empathic mode of perception about my supervisee's dilemma. I then learned that the emerging disavowed childhood feelings of the patient were being powerfully replicated in my supervisee's internal world, and had a disorganizing impact on him. The missing links to the patient's material directly corresponded to the earlier selfobject failures the supervisee had experienced, and proved to be a major impediment in his ability to tolerate and subsequently organize his experience around the patient's affect. In addition, my supervisee's extreme vulnerability to any affect from the patient rendered him unable to provide any sustained, attuned responsiveness or selfobject experience in the treatment.

Once this understanding was established it became clear to me that the most basic aspect of our work together was primarily to provide the supervisee with a mirroring selfobject experience. My failure began when I gave priority to the vantage point of the patient in the relationship, and denied my supervisee the experience of my empathy for his experience.

I had to reevaluate and reorganize the purpose of our supervisory meetings. After consistently providing a mirroring selfobject experience for the supervisee, there appeared to be a significant reduction of his fragmentation anxiety. Over time, without having to specifically articulate to my supervisee the obvious parallel or over-identification with his patient, the supervisory atmosphere created enough safety for him to consider the parallel meaning between his experience and the patient's experience and then to differentiate from the patient's experience. He began to identify his own unresolved issues around the integration of affect, and I believe it had a therapeutic value. It provided a less dangerous path of indirectly taking in newfound knowledge around the problems about his learning without feeling criticized or overly exposed. The supervisee's experience of working through a developmental phase in the supervision assisted him in developing an ability to self-articulate, differentiate his meaning from the patient's meaning, and heightened his awareness of how to self-regulate his affective responses to the patient's material. The provision of a much-needed mirroring and idealizing selfobject experience for the supervisee promoted self-cohesion. This working-through phase of the supervisee's problems about learning eventuated in his re-gaining a sense of efficacy and competence, and created a vitaliz-ing selfobject experience.

DEVELOPING A WORKING ALLIANCE

It is characteristic of the analyst-in-training to experience, at one time or another, several if not all of the selfobject transferences that coincide with their particular developmental phases of learn-ing. For example, the alter-ego selfobject experience will very often occur as a result of a need to feel a part of a peer group in class or group supervision. This alter-ego selfobject experience can have a stabilizing effect even while the individual supervision does not appear to be providing a selfobject experience for the student. In addition there is a continuing need for some students to feel iden-tified with and internalize idealized teachers, values, and theoreti-cal constructs that then serve a selfobject function. This is not to be confused with certain characterological resistances that can emerge in psychoanalytic supervision, for example, the narcissistic collusion between supervisor and supervisee in which both parties do not feel free to give the other honest feedback (Glickauf-Hughes 1994). In contrast, if these selfobject needs of the analyst-in-training are met, a more accepting ambiance will emerge and then increase the possibility for a co-participating ambiance and will create a space for reflection and dialogue (Fosshage 1997).

Developing a working alliance with the supervisee may consist primarily of the task of understanding the nature of the selfobject experience needed in order to facilitate the learning. Investigating and being responsive to the selfobject needs of the supervisee involves empathic attunement and an educational awareness about his particular developmental needs as it relates to his problems about learning. Implementing Wolf's (1995) understanding of the "disruption–restoration sequence" assists us in applying this very central position in self psychology to restoring the bond between teacher and student when an empathic failure has occurred in supervision.

One of the most basic aspects of supervision is the reduction of the supervisee's anxiety and the promotion of self-esteem and self-cohesion. By providing a stabilizing selfobject experience for the supervisee, the supervisor is directly or indirectly attending to the supervisee's momentary disequilibrium in order to facilitate an optimal learning environment (Fosshage 1997).

REFERENCES

Brightman, B. (1984). Narcissistic issues in the training experience of the psychotherapist. *International Journal of Psychoanalytic Psychotherapy* 10:293–317.

Epstein, L. (1986). Collusive selective inattention to the negative impact of the supervisory interaction. *Contemporary Psychoanalysis* 22:389–417.

Fosshage, J. (1997). Toward a model of psychoanalytic supervision from a self psychological/intersubjective perspective. In *Psy-*

chodynamic Supervision, ed. M. Rock, pp. 189–210. Northvale, NJ: Jason Aronson.

Glickauf-Hughes, C. (1994). Characterological resistances in psychotherapy supervision. *Psychotherapy* 31:58–66.

Jacobs, D., David, P., and Meyer, D. (1995). *The Supervisory Encounter.* New Haven, CT: Yale University Press.

Kohut, H. (1971). *The Analysis of the Self.* New York: International Universities Press.

———. (1978) *The Search for the Self: Selected Writings of Heinz Kohut: 1950–1978.* New York: International Universities Press.

———. (1984). *How Does Analysis Cure?* Chicago: University of Chicago Press.

Lichtenberg, J. (1983). *Psychoanalysis and Infant Research.* Hillsdale, NJ: Analytic Press.

Lichtenberg, J., Lachmann, F., and Fosshage, J. (1992). *Self and Motivational Systems.* Hillsdale, NJ: Analytic Press.

Rock, M., ed. (1997). Effective supervision. In *Psychodynamic Supervision,* pp. 107–132. Northvale, NJ: Jason Aronson.

Stern, D. (1985). *The Interpersonal World of the Infant.* New York: Basic Books.

Stolorow, R., Brandchaft, B., and Atwood, G. (1987). *Psychoanalytic Treatment: An Intersubjective Approach.* Hillsdale, NJ: Analytic Press.

Teitelbaum, S. (1998). The impact of the supervisory style. *Psychoanalysis and Psychotherapy* 15:115–129.

Wolf, E. (1980). On the developmental line of selfobject relations. In *Advances in Self Psychology,* ed. A. Goldberg, pp. 117–130. New York: International Universities Press.

———. (1988). *Treating the Self.* New York: Guilford.

———. (1994). Selfobject experiences: development, psychopathology, treatment. In *Mahler and Kohut: Perspectives on Development, Psychopathology, and Technique,* ed. S. Kramer and S. Akhtar, pp. 65–96. Northvale, NJ: Jason Aronson.

———. (1995). How to supervise without doing harm: comments on psychoanalytic supervision. *Psychoanalytic Inquiry* 15:252–267.

9

How Does Supervision Teach?[1]

MARY BETH M. CRESCI

The adage, "Those who can, do. Those who can't, teach," is fortunately not applicable to the profession of psychoanalysis. Most psychoanalysts who teach and supervise at a psychoanalytic institute or in their private practice do so as a sideline to their primary work as psychoanalysts. The fact that psychoanalysts are both "doing" and "teaching-supervising" at the same time is a great advantage in enabling the supervisor to appreciate more fully the learning needs of the supervisee and the difficult tasks she is undertaking. Presumably, from her own work the supervisor will have many insights and points of information with which to help the supervisee learn.

On the other hand, the disadvantage of this apprenticeship model is that often the master teacher-supervisor has not specifi-

---

1. An earlier version of this chapter was presented at the Division 39 conference, American Psychoanalytic Association, April 14, 1994.

cally learned how to impart knowledge or skills to another. Our own training focuses on becoming psychoanalysts, not on becoming teachers and supervisors. While a master carpenter may be able to simply demonstrate his skills to his apprentice, the necessities of privacy and confidentiality preclude the use of demonstration in most cases of psychoanalytic supervision. The psychoanalyst-supervisor must rely on verbal communication in the form of listening, providing information, questioning, suggesting, criticizing, and so on to learn what the supervisee is doing and to help her do it better.

Furthermore, there is the additional task of determining what the supervisor may want to teach and whether it is relevant to the supervisee. Ekstein and Wallerstein (1980) refer to the dilemma of teaching "creative expression" versus "technical skills" (p. 4). They suggest that a learner-supervisee needs the opportunity not only to learn technical know-how but also to develop her own unique capacities as a psychoanalyst. The need for creative expression may be hampered in the apprenticeship supervisory model when the master craftsman-supervisor has particular theoretical or technical positions she wants the supervisee to follow. In addition, as a senior member of the guild system, the supervisor is seen as the authority and final judge of the supervisee's work.

The supervisor's expectations of the supervisee and the supervisor's theoretical orientation may affect the supervisor's determination of what the supervisee has actually learned in supervision. Just as the supervisor cannot simply demonstrate her psychoanalytic skills to the supervisee, so the supervisor cannot directly observe the supervisee's work with the patient. The supervisor learns of the supervisee's work generally through the reading of process notes and self-report, methods that can easily be selective in presenting those aspects that the supervisee wants to reveal. Oftentimes, the supervisor has her own particular ideas to convey and is judging the supervisee's work from that predetermined perspective.

On the other hand, the supervisee's awareness of how much she has learned is also quite subjective. The supervisee may find the supervisor's suggestions helpful or off the mark. She may see ways in which the supervision has improved her work or feel it is at best irrelevant. In fact, this chapter will seek to demonstrate that the overriding factor that determines whether a supervisee feels she has learned from supervision is the extent to which she feels reasonably comfortable and not overly anxious during the supervision.

THE SUBJECTIVE NATURE OF SUPERVISION

The difficulties of determining what really transpires in supervision and what enables a supervisee to learn have been borne out as I have observed supervisor demonstrations during a series of conferences at the Postgraduate Center for Mental Health. The demonstrations were conducted by several highly experienced analysts from a variety of theoretical orientations. Although the conferences had a number of themes, mainly focusing on how supervision might vary depending on different theoretical orientations of the supervisor, they all provided an opportunity to observe directly rather than through summary reports what the supervisor wanted to teach, what form the supervision took, and how successfully the supervisee learned from the experience.

In comparing my own observations of the demonstrations with those of the supervisor and the supervisee participants and other members of the audience, I was struck by the wide discrepancies among these three groups in understanding what had happened during the supervision. It was as though we were the proverbial blind men trying to describe an elephant. Sometimes the observation of the verbal and nonverbal cues of the supervisee during the supervision were substantially different from the supervisee's later evaluation of his experience. Also, quite often many members of the audience had reactions to the quality of the supervision that were markedly different from the participants' reactions and from each other. Depending on which data were accepted as most valid, the assessment of the learning that occurred varied dramatically.

The format that was used for the two conferences involved asking two experienced supervisors with different theoretical orientations each to conduct a supervisory session with the same supervisee. The supervisee was asked to present the same patient and same process material to both supervisors. There were remarkable differences in the two supervisory sessions at both conferences.

CASE EXAMPLE 1

In the first conference the female supervisee presented a young female analytic patient who was very dissatisfied with her life. The material presented by the supervisee indicated that the patient was locked in struggles with both parents over their expectations for her success both professionally and in her choice of a suitable husband. The supervisee seemed to feel at an impasse in the treatment, unable to help the patient identify what was really bothering her and constructively work on it. In her presentation, the supervisee had been asked by the supervisor first to read a short statement describing the patient, including presenting problems, early history, and course of treatment to date, and then to read a verbatim transcript of a recent session.

The first supervisor was a Freudian. After the supervisee had read the description of the patient and the session transcript, the supervisor stated that he thought it would be most helpful to the supervisee if he were to review the description of the patient and discuss the patient in terms of the psychosexual stages of development that were evident in this description. Thus, he reviewed the written page about the patient and pointed out how the material could be seen as derivatives or symbols of oral, anal, phallic, and genital issues. The focus was almost exclusively on understanding the patient's dynamics with practically no reference to the patient–therapist interaction or to understanding the impasse that the supervisee was experiencing.

The second supervisor was an interpersonal analyst. He chose to go directly to the session material and attempted to explore the supervisee's feelings and reactions as the session progressed. He picked up on sighs or frowns the supervisee made during the supervision or reported from the analytic session. Soon the supervisor had the supervisee describing the session as a boxing match and the patient as a feisty sparring partner who slipped punches and was very difficult to engage directly. He then encouraged her to think of ways to help the two protagonists, patient and supervisee-analyst, to take off their gloves and be more cooperative in their efforts. The supervisee found it very difficult to imagine how this goal could be accomplished. She asked the supervisor for suggestions of how to stop the boxing match. However, the supervisor did not provide her with answers. Instead, he continually turned the question back around and encouraged her to look further at her own experience with the patient.

The supervisee's reactions during and after the two sessions suggested that she felt more comfortable during the session with the Freudian supervisor and, initially at least, felt she learned more in that format. She made several comments during that supervision, for instance, to agree with a point the Freudian supervisor made about the patient and to extend it to something else in her work with the patient. She frequently nodded her head and took notes. The interpersonal supervisor asked the supervisee more questions about her feelings and reactions to the patients. At times, she responded quickly and with enthusiasm, particularly in expressing some pent-up frustration and anger. However, late in the supervision, when she asked the supervisor for his ideas, she seemed annoyed that he did not give her more suggestions for understanding her dilemma with the patient and solving it. She seemed to be frustrated by the supervisor as much as she was by the patient, thereby suggesting that a parallel process was occurring in which the supervisee experienced with the supervisor a boxing match similar to the one she was having with the patient in the therapy session. In both cases, her opponents were "slipping punches" and not engaging directly with her.

If we were to consider the learning that occurred in these two supervision sessions primarily from the in-session responsiveness and immediate post-session reactions of the supervisee, we might conclude that the supervisee had learned much more in the first supervision with the Freudian supervisor. However, in general, the audience had a different reaction. They tended to find the first supervision session overly didactic and not sufficiently responsive to the supervisee's needs and experience. They felt some of the frustration the supervisee expressed in the second supervision with the interpersonal supervisor but saw potential in that approach for the supervisee to begin to understand what the impasse in the treatment was all about. The supervisee herself said at a much later date that the second supervisory approach had been very alien to her at the time, but that she could imagine learning more from it had she been better prepared to work in that manner.

CASE EXAMPLE 2

In the second supervisory conference with a similar format, the male supervisee presented a young male patient who was in both individual and group treatment with him. The patient was strongly attached to a sister and worried that he tended to try to garner her approval, as well as the approval of others, by conforming to others' viewpoints and losing his own sense of individuality. In this conference the wide variation between a supervisor who concentrated almost exclusively on the patient's dynamics and one who focused almost exclusively on the supervisee's experience was not as evident. Nevertheless, differences in the supervision occurred in more subtle form.

The first supervisor had a Freudian orientation. The format again called for the supervisee to describe the patient briefly and then present verbatim session notes. More than any of the other supervisors, this Freudian supervisor made an immediate effort to establish a rapport with the supervisee. He shook the supervisee's hand, encouraged him to sit down and relax, and suggested that he present the material in his own way. The supervisee's body posture was relaxed and there was much nodding and responsiveness between the two participants. The supervisor showed a considerable interest in understanding the patient's dynamics but did this more in the context of looking at transference manifestations in the session than had the Freudian supervisor in the first conference. Thus, even though one of the supervisors at each conference had a Freudian orientation, they chose very different material to focus on with the supervisees.

As the supervisee began to present verbatim material to the Freudian supervisor, he reported that the patient early in the session brought up a criticism that a group member had made about the patient in a previous group session. The patient then asked the therapist-supervisee whether he agreed with the criticism. The Freudian supervisor quickly understood that the patient had not felt sufficiently supported and protected by the supervisee during the group session and that this had raised important transference issues which now needed to be addressed in the individual therapy session. The supervisor commented on a number of the supervisee's interventions regarding their aptness in addressing the underlying transference dynamics. In each case the tone was one of suggesting that, given this patient's dynamics, the supervisee's comments were bound to be experienced negatively or unsupportively. Thus, the onus of blame for moments when the supervisee's comments were not on the mark was taken off the supervisee and placed on the patient, so that a collegial, noncritical relationship was maintained throughout the supervision.

In the second supervisory session, the supervisee presented the same material to a supervisor who is noted for her focus on the use of empathic listening. She requested that the supervisee first read the session through completely and that then they would go back to the beginning and review it in detail. The supervisee clearly felt uncomfortable with this approach. He seemed to feel that much of the control would be taken out of his hands since he could not present the material as he preferred to do with his own commentary interspersed with the reading. In addressing the material, the supervisor focused on the degree to which the supervisee was not listening to the patient. She indicated that the supervisee was instead setting his own agenda and directing the patient to the issues that the supervisee wanted him to address. A parallel process of sorts occurred as the supervisor established her agenda in the supervision session in a similar fashion to the supervisee's alleged tendency to follow his own agenda with the patient.

The supervisee's reaction afterwards to the two supervisory 'sessions was to express judiciously more positive feelings toward the supervisor with whom he apparently felt more comfortable, the Freudian supervisor. The audience corroborated in enjoying the collegial atmosphere they observed and in believing the Freudian supervisor had more readily identified a transference issue of importance to the treatment. On the other hand, some observers were concerned that so much of the focus remained with the patient as the cause of the resistance and the therapeutic impasse. The audience had negative reactions to what they observed to be the controlling style of the empathic-listening supervisor. They apparently identified with the discomfort the supervisee showed during the session via many nonverbal cues.

FACILITATING THE SUPERVISEE'S LEARNING

From the description of the supervisory sessions, it seems clear that, regardless of the audience's opinions, both supervisees felt they learned more in the session in which they were more relaxed and comfortable. Sessions in which their interventions were subject to criticism or their countertransference was addressed directly made them feel exposed and increased their anxiety levels. Naturally, these feelings are heightened when the supervision occurs in a public forum. Nevertheless, they do not seem antithetical to supervision occurring in a private office, especially when there is an evaluative component to supervision that is conducted under the auspices of an analytic training institute. The fact that the supervisee is being observed and evaluated in any supervisory venue makes this fact an inevitable aspect of the learning situation, which must be taken into consideration by the supervisor.

Several authors (most notable, Epstein 1986, Lesser 1983) have discussed collusion in which the supervisee's negative reactions are not addressed in supervisory relationships. Epstein (1986), for instance, discusses a supervisee who terminated abruptly after about eight sessions even though Epstein felt he was doing a great deal to help the supervisee improve his work with his patients. He concluded that, while he was enabling him to do better work, he had not done enough to help the supervisee explore his own feelings of inadequacy with the patient. In his discussion of the Epstein article, Feiner (1986) suggests that a destructive form of competitive envy was in operation here such that Epstein's supervisory success in understanding the patient and knowing what to do only increased the supervisee's own feelings of inadequacy.

Epstein (1986) calls the normal supervisory format a tutorial one in which the supervisor gains access to the supervisee's knowledge and interventions and gives the supervisee advice and insights to improve his capacities. He points to the negative impact this model may have on the supervisee, since it focuses on what the supervisee doesn't know and what the supervisor does know. He suggests several alterations that can be made to the tutorial model. The two basic revisions he suggests are (1) to "make a conscious effort to focus no less of (the supervisor's) interest and attention on the supervisee than his work with patients," specifically, the supervisee's feelings and reactions to both the supervisory and treatment situation; and (2) for the supervisor to practice "active-participant-observation," meaning that the supervisor must be "consistently alert to the impact of his personality style, his interventions, and of the entire supervisory process on the supervisee" (pp. 397–398).

In discussing the specifics of this approach, it becomes clear that Epstein focuses on the supervisee's reactions to the supervision for the express purpose of determining the supervisee's gradient of anxiety and doing what he can to alleviate an excessive level of anxiety. He does this by encouraging the supervisee to express his negative feelings toward both the supervisor and the patient, and taking as much responsibility as he can as a supervisor for failures in the treatment. He believes that ultimately this approach will enable the supervisee to be more tolerant of his own mistakes and to be able to openly discuss his difficulties and need for a greater understanding and technical skill.

Feiner's response to Epstein makes the interesting caveat that not all envy need be so competitive and destructive. He cites his own work with eminent supervisors from whom he learned a great deal and did not feel diminished in the process. Possibly, there are ways by which the supervisee can experience the supervision as enabling him to become more like the supervisor such that he does not find the supervisor's knowledge to be so threatening to his own worth. He may, in fact, develop an "interactive identification" with the supervisor, as Tansey and Burke (1989) suggest the therapist develops with his patient, which will assist him in being open to the supervisor's point of view rather than experiencing it as assaultive. Epstein suggests that the supervisor must actively work to take inordinate responsibility for failure so that the supervisee does not feel denigrated. His position may be an extreme one and may suggest undue distortion of the supervisory situation. However, many supervisors may use other, less externalizing stances that reduce anxiety levels and increase the supervisee's self-esteem in an admittedly difficult learning situation.

If we move away from the perspective of working as supervisors to our underlying role as analysts, some of the points made by Epstein and Feiner regarding supervisors and supervisees can be compared to aspects of the analytic relationship between patient and analyst. Beginning with Freud's (1912) emphasis on the rapport, which is a helpful aspect of the patient's positive transference to the analyst, other classical analysts such as Greenson (1967) have described the importance of establishing a working alliance at the beginning of treatment. Greenson has emphasized that it is not possible for a patient to benefit from interpretations before the patient has accepted the basic position that he and the analyst are working together on his behalf to understand his problems. Analysts often consider the establishment of the working alliance to be in part their responsibility as they carefully choose initial interpretations with the goals of piquing the patient's interest regarding their intrapsychic life and genetic history and of educating the patient about the analytic process itself. They, too, are concerned with establishing an optimal level of anxiety which is neither so overwhelming nor so absent that work cannot be accomplished in the analysis.

Alternatively, self psychologists have discussed different aspects of transference that create a variety of selfobject bounds between the analyst and patient. In serving mirroring, idealizing, or twinship selfobject functions, the analyst enables the patient to overcome anxiety and feel a rapport with the analyst.

Both of these concepts borrowed from the analytic relationship, namely, the concept of the working alliance and the concept of the selfobject function served by the transference in self psychology terms, may be at the base of Epstein's observation of the need to attend to the supervisory relationship itself. Certainly, Epstein is focusing on what the analyst would call the working alliance when he suggests asking the supervisee for his reactions to the supervision. Similarly, he fulfills a variety of selfobject functions when he approves of a supervisee's interventions with a patient or suggests that he may need to be more helpful to the supervisee if there are problems in the treatment with the patient. In these cases he is mirroring the supervisee or trying to establish a twinship or an idealization to counteract the competitive envy that can derail the supervision. Epstein is not advocating interpreting the transference, to borrow again from the analytic relationship, but is instead using the positive aspects of the transference to further the supervision and attempting to minimize the negative transference.

To return to the four supervisory sessions described above, we can see why the apparent comfort of the supervisee in the various sessions was so highly correlated with the supervisee's sense that he or she had learned something in the supervision. The optimal level of anxiety may have been achieved in the second conference between the male supervisee and the Freudian supervisor. In that case, the supervisor addressed specific process material in the therapy sessions and considered ways in which the patient's transference might have been better understood and addressed. Session material that could have been anxiety-producing because it exposed the supervisee's difficulties was certainly discussed. However, the supervisor used several techniques to make sure that the supervisee's anxiety did not increase precipitously. He specifically made efforts to establish a collegial, respectful rapport with the supervisee, and he tended to blame the patient's transference difficulties or inevitable aspects of the process itself for whatever impasses were evident in the therapy session. Thus, the supervisee did not have to feel criticized for mistakes in his work. The supervisor did not take the path of encouraging the supervisee to blame the supervisor for lack of progress in the supervision, as Epstein advocates. Instead, he uses the patient's pathology as a way to externalize the difficulties in the treatment and keep any criticism from overwhelming the supervisee.

The session that the same supervisee had with the empathic-listening supervisor more closely approximates Epstein's description of tutorial supervision. The supervisor looked directly at the supervisee's interventions with the patient and established a focus which implied that it was the supervisee's responsibility to follow the patient. The supervisor was seen as the expert who could identify the points at which the supervisee deviated from the patient's focus. She could then suggest alternative interventions to improve the supervisee's listening skills. Thus, blame for failure to listen was placed squarely on the supervisee's shoulders, not on the supervisor's or the patient's.

In the first conference the interpersonal supervisor established a neutral position in which the boxing match between the supervisee and her patient was not necessarily anyone's fault. Nor did the supervisor imply that he was the expert with the answers as the tutorial model of supervision would require. Nevertheless, highlighting the therapeutic impasse without suggesting a way out tended to put the responsibility back on the shoulders of the supervisee. Her confusion and lack of satisfaction with the supervisor's answers to her questions thus raised the gradient of anxiety higher than the supervisee could tolerate and impeded the learning process. A particular consideration with this supervision was that the supervisee was unfamiliar with the interpersonal theoretical position and the focus that a supervisor working from this position might take.

This fact promotes the observation that supervisees at different levels of development and with different prior experience in supervision may be able to benefit from one style of supervision more than another. The optimal learning situation may change as the supervisee develops. The supervisee in the first conference, for instance, might have found the Freudian supervisor's didactic style informative and helpful initially. Certainly, she showed less anxiety during this supervision and expressed more satisfaction with it during that conference. However, if this approach had not eventually focused more directly on her interventions and her transference–countertransference dilemmas, the supervisee might well have ultimately become dissatisfied with the supervision. In contrast, the supervisee in time might have felt it less necessary to obtain specific answers from the interpersonal supervisor and been more interested in exploring her own perceptions and understanding much as the interpersonal supervisor was encouraging her to do. The didactic and open-ended supervisory styles may, indeed, be formats which are effective at different stages in the supervisory relationship as well as at different stages in the supervisee's own professional development.

In conclusion, the amount of learning reported to occur in a given supervisory experience depends on who is making the report and the criteria being used to evaluate the experience. A supervisee seems to base her estimate of the supervision on the degree to which she feels relaxed and engaged in the supervision and on the degree to which she does not feel anxious and criticized. There seems to be an optimal level at which the supervisee is engaged and working and yet not excessively anxious. To help the supervisee achieve this level, the supervisor can actively strive to achieve a collegial relationship and to monitor the supervisee's level of anxiety. The supervisor can attempt to alleviate high levels of anxiety by encouraging the supervisee to discuss her feelings about the patient and the supervisor and by assuming responsibility for difficulties in the supervision or with the patient. Ultimately, the supervisor hopes that the supervisee herself will be able to internalize the capacity to evaluate her own work in a creative, nonjudgmental manner. The supervisor's readiness to have the supervisee evaluate the supervisor's work and to give the supervisee's comments serious consideration is an important precursor to the supervisee's ability to become an active participant and learner in the supervisory process.

REFERENCES

Ekstein, R., and Wallerstein, R. (1980). *The Teaching and Learning of Psychotherapy*. New York: International Universities Press.

Epstein, L. (1986). Collusive selective inattention to the negative impact of the supervisory interaction. *Contemporary Psychoanalysis* 22:389–409.

Feiner, A. (1986). Discussion. *Contemporary Psychoanalysis* 22:409–417.

Freud, S. (1912). The dynamics of transference. *Standard Edition* 12:97–108.

Greenson, R. (1967). *The Technique and Practice of Psychoanalysis*. New York: International Universities Press.

Lesser, R. M. (1983). Supervision: illusions, anxieties, and questions. *Contemporary Psychoanalysis* 19:120–129.

Tansey, M., and Burke, W. (1989). *Understanding Countertransference: From Projective Identification to Empathy*. Hillsdale, NJ: Analytic Press.

II

Working with Countertransference

10

Collusive Selective Inattention to the Negative Impact of the Supervisory Interaction[1,2]

LAWRENCE EPSTEIN

It has become increasingly clear to me that the traditional tutorial psychoanalytic supervisory relationship, because of its authoritarian tilt, may easily lead both participants to collude in a process of selective inattention. This collusion is to indications of the negative impact of supervision on the supervisee and on his functioning with the patient under supervision. My aim in this chapter is to identify and discuss those features of supervisory practice that are likely to disadvantage the supervisee and the treatment relationship, to suggest how the supervisory rela-

1. This chapter is a revised and expanded version of a paper presented both at a joint meeting of the Adelphi Society of Psychoanalysis and Psychotherapy and the Long Island Institute of Psychoanalysis in January, 1984 and at a workshop conference of the International Forum of Psychoanalysis in Madrid in September, 1984.

2. I want to thank Dr. Irwin Hirsch for his critical commentary and his useful suggestions.

tionship might be conducted so as to minimize its potential for negative influence, and to limit the development within the relationship of tacit agreements to take no notice of signs of this influence.

Fiscalini (1985) has discussed the issue of parataxic interferences in the supervisory relationship. He derives his understanding of such interferences mainly from a retrospective review of the varying impact of two successive supervisory relationships on himself and on his treatment of the same patient during the period that Fiscalini was a candidate in psychoanalytic training. The first supervisor focused mainly on Fiscalini's failures to confront "the patient's hostile security operations and his self-centered disregard for others" (p. 594). Fiscalini writes, "My initial sympathy with the patient's plight and empathic feel for his anxiety were gradually submerged in a one-sided emphasis on his hostile and alienating defensive operations" (p. 594). Fiscalini's second supervisor

> soon diagnosed the parataxic difficulty between the patient and myself, helping me to see the impact of my anxiety and anger on the analytic relationship. . . . In the supervisory situation, the supervisor focused on my anxiety in the analysis. . . . As I became more secure in the analytic relationship and in supervision and grapsed my parataxic participation in both, the analytic inquiry became broader and deeper . . . and in time, the patient began to show genuine concern and sympathy for others in his life and he became better able to see them and himself realistically. [p. 596]

It is striking that the actual emotional impact of the supervisor's conduct of the supervision on the supervisee and on its carryover to the supervisee's conduct of the treatment has received scant attention in the psychoanalytic literature. It has been mentioned but not elaborated, in papers by Searles (1962) and Gediman and Wolkenfeld (1980).

The subject has, however, been studied in depth by Doehrman (1976) in a setting for the training of clinical psychologists.

Among Doehrman's conclusions, the following are noteworthy:

> if [the] transference–countertransference binds which developed in the supervisory relationship had not been recognized and worked through, the supervisory and therapeutic process would have suffered. Supervision had become something more than a didactic or consultative experience. . . . It seems reasonable . . . to generalize that all supervisors should be extremely sensitive to unknown and intense effects that they will have upon their supervisees, as well as the effects their supervisees may have upon them, and not assume that their relationship with a trainee is a simple didactic one. . . . Almost exactly at the points where the resolutions of the transference binds in the supervisor–therapist relationships occurred, resolutions of the transference binds in the therapist–patient relationships also occurred and the emotional climate of both relationships changed. [p. 76]

A candidate-in-training recently provided me with a clear example of such "unknown and intense effects" of supervisor upon supervisee.

> During a session with his patient, the supervisee found himself unable to concentrate on what the patient was talking about. His attention kept drifting away and he found himself preoccupied with personal concerns. Unable to bring this process of involuntary distraction to a halt, he decided to associate to the problem. He recalled his experience of the last supervisory session in which this patient was discussed. At a certain point in the session, his supervisor began to talk about his own work with a similar patient. The candidate remembered feeling slightly unsettled by this but resolved the matter by thinking to himself, "Oh, that's good. He's treating me like a peer." It came to him, while associating, that he had actually suppressed feelings

of being emotionally abandoned by his supervisor, and he then understood that he had been unwittingly and uncontrollably subjecting his patient to similar mistreatment.

In this example, the impact of the supervisor's empathic failure was apparently so subtle as to lead the supervisee to suppress his negative thoughts and feelings so that they remained at the level of unformulated experience (see Stern 1983).

I think it is reasonable to infer from this example, as well as from Fiscalini's experience and Doehrman's research, that the treatment relationship is likely to be especially vulnerable to a carryover of negative impact from the supervisory relationship when the supervisee's experience of such negative impact is unformulated. In order to limit the development of this problem, or to correct for it, it would be important for the supervisor to develop a relationship with the supervisee in which the supervisee is enabled, with a minimal sense of risk, to contact and put into words whatever negative thoughts and feelings he may be experiencing vis-à-vis the supervisor or the supervision.

In the traditional tutorial supervisory relationship, the supervisor is generally not interested in the problem of his potential negative impact. Such information may actually be unwelcome. Should the supervisor have an aversion to discovering any negative impact he might be having, the supervisee is likely to join him in a tacit collusion to be selectively inattentive to such matters.[3]

My own awareness of the problem of collusive selective inattention as a pitfall of the traditional tutorial supervisory relationship has emerged mainly from experiences of supervisory failure and near-failure and from my participation in the process of group supervision both as a group member and as a group supervisor.

---

3. Lesser (1983) stresses the importance of the supervisor's conducting "an in-depth inquiry into and analysis of each member's transferences and countertransferences which are directly experienced by and observable to one another. . ." (p. 127).

Before discussing those features of group supervision which both limit the operation of selective inattention and facilitate awareness of subtle signs of negative supervisory impact, I want to define what I mean by the traditional tutorial supervisory relationship and to discuss its built-in pitfalls.

THE TRADITIONAL TUTORIAL MODEL

In this model, following the model of my own supervisors, I would monitor my supervisee's treatment of his patient, teaching him to listen for derivatives of unconscious processes and to understand the genetic and dynamic meaning and function of variations in the transference. I would call attention to subjective countertransference interferences and help the supervisee identify the objective component of the countertransference experience and to learn how to address this component as data in order to better understand the patient's ongoing unconscious processes. I would routinely call attention to lapses in maintaining the treatment frame, to failures to set appropriate limits, to errors of intervention, to lapses of observation and understanding, and to lost opportunities for making facilitating interventions. I would confront the supervisee with such resistances to the supervisory process as came to my attention: lateness, absences, sloppy preparation, desultory presentation of material, and so on.

The implicit definition of tasks in this tutorial approach would seem to be the following: the supervisor's task is to guide, advise, and teach, by informing, correcting, challenging and confronting; the supervisee's task is to learn, and it is hoped the supervisee's analyst will deal with those characterological or neurotic problems that constitute interferences to the supervisee's capability for assimilating and integrating his supervision experience.

The main focus of this approach is the patient–therapist relationship. As the patient becomes more difficult to treat and/or as the supervisee shows himself to be more at a loss as to how to treat his patient, the supervisor, should he follow his natural inclinations to get the therapy situation under control, will be increasingly found to attempt to influence the supervisee to treat the patient as he, himself, would. Thus supervision can easily become a process in which the supervisor attempts to treat the patient through the supervisee. (Fiscalini [1985] has aptly termed this "analysis by ventriloquism.") Should such be the case, the needs and feelings of the patient become more important to the supervisor than the needs and feelings of the supervisee, with ensuing negative effects.

In the traditional supervisory context neither the concept nor the practice of participant-observation seems to apply to the supervisor's conduct of the supervision. Both participants, therefore, are likely to be selectively inattentive to any negative impact that the supervisory process might be having.

AN EXPERIENCE OF SUPERVISORY FAILURE

I was consulted by an analyst who, a year earlier, was graduated from an institute in which he said he had been exposed to varying and somewhat diverging points of view regarding both theory and practice. He said that since graduating he had been in a state of confusion. He wanted help in gaining a clearer grasp of the analytic process. He no longer wanted to operate "by the seat of his pants." He felt especially ineffective in treating a number of difficult borderline patients. He was consulting me because he had heard from others who had taken classes and supervision with me that I had an effective approach to treating such patients and that in my approach I had integrated different points of view. He also hoped to get some help in dealing with his countertransference.

When the supervisee began to present cases, it became clear immediately that things were much as he had said they were. Because he had little understanding of the resistances presented by his difficult patients, he was very frustrated and intervened ineffectively under the sway of intense negative countertransference feelings.

I found him very easy to supervise. He was very cooperative with my suggestions for getting the cases he was presenting under control.

One case in particular was upsetting to him and was, in fact, going very badly. A married female patient complained incessantly and repetitiously about the way people in her life were treating her. She frustrated all of his efforts to get her interested in understanding anything, and when she wasn't complaining, she talked trivia. In his efforts to get her to make some sort of meaningful connections, the supervisee invariably found himself in a sadomasochistic interaction. He found himself criticizing her and attempting to control her, sometimes verging on being punitive. He felt guilty and terrible about himself as a therapist. I explained that the patient was using the same passive-aggressive tactics with the supervisee that she had used all of her life with her mother, and that she was currently using with her husband, and that these tactics came into play whenever she was found wanting or was criticized. I suggested that the patient probably needed, at this time, to use the therapy sessions as an emotional toilet into which she could evacuate her accumulated emotional debris and, should that be the case, she needed the therapist to do nothing more for the time being than tolerate the situation. I suggested that the face-to-face situation was probably overstimulating to this patient and that she would probably feel more relaxed and be less troublesome on the couch. I suggested that, for the time being, the supervisee make no interpretations, nor ask probing questions, nor attempt to get the patient to understand that she wasn't interested in understanding. I suggested too that he restrict his interventions either to occasional comments reflecting some empathic understanding of the patient's feelings or to questions that had only the purpose of clarifying some information given by the patient.

The supervisee followed my suggestions. He no longer felt provoked to treat his patient sadistically, and her functioning in her life showed progressive improvement. The supervisee, however, felt very uncomfortable with this way of practicing. He complained that he did not feel like an analyst with his patient, that he felt useless and that it made no sense to him that the patient should progress in such a context. He felt like a fraud and, out of his need to feel legitimate, he felt strong urges to explain to the patient what I had explained to him about this toilet situation. I told him that the patient would be unlikely to welcome such information, that she would probably feel criticized and that he might soon find himself treating her sadistically. I told him that he had two un-gratifying choices: to feel like a useless fraud or to feel like a sadist, and that it would be better for his patient if he chose the former. I explained that at this stage of the treatment his patient, in order to feel secure and comfortable, apparently needed to feel in con-trol of the treatment relationship. She needed the therapist, for the time being, to function as a selfobject rather than as a separate per-son with a mind of his own. His countertransference reactions of feeling underemployed or useless were, therefore, nothing more than the normal counterpart of his patient's selfobject transference. Sooner or later, I said, when his patient was more ready to bring her aggression out into the open, she would probably begin to find fault with his lack of input. He would then be in a good position to investigate what other interventions might be of use.

In a similar way, I helped the supervisee with his other diffi-cult treatment situations. For the most part, he got them under control, and his patients were doing well.

At the end of the eighth session, the supervisee, giving me some reason that I did not believe, informed me that he was un-able to continue supervision at this time. He thanked me for the help I had given him and said that he would like to return at a later date. That was many years ago and he never again contacted me for supervision.

My first reaction was to feel both terrible about myself and intense anger and contempt for the supervisee. When I asked myself what it was that I had done wrong, the answer was embar-rassingly simple. While I was focused on helping this supervisee to function effectively with his patients, I neglected his more basic problem, namely, his complex of terrible feelings about himself as a therapist. In being so successful in helping him with his patients, I failed to consider the possibility that I was making him feel so stupid and inadequate about his analytic understanding and therapeutic skill that he probably came to find the supervision unbearably painful. It might have made the situation more emotionally tolerable for my supervisee had I—before displaying my quick and confident understanding of his induced countertransference— taken his complaints about feeling fraudulent and useless seriously enough to investigate them thoroughly and empathically.[4]

My own bad feelings about this fiasco are eased somewhat by a feeling of camaraderie with Freud (1905). I am reminded of his being cut off by Dora at the peak of his analytic potency after less than three months of treatment. The problem was that whatever Dora might have felt she wanted or needed was irrelevant to Freud. According to Erickson (1964), Dora needed Freud to affirm the actuality of her experience of having been so ill-used as an adolescent by the significant adults in her life. As Freud saw it, what Dora needed was the analysis of her unconscious conflicts.

My supervisee's need to have his low self-esteem as an analyst taken into account was for me irrelevant to the project of teaching him how to do more effective therapeutic work.

GROUP SUPERVISION

Now let me describe group supervision as I have experienced it as a group member and as I now conduct it as a group supervisor. The work is done on two levels. The supervisees present current

---

4. My conclusion concerning the main reason for my supervisee's abrupt termination has been criticized as taking insufficient account of other possible motives. In the absence of any confirmatory data, this criticism is, of course, warranted. The issue of the rightness or wrongness of my conclusion, however, is of less importance to me than its value in alerting me to the ever-present possibility of my negative impact.

cases with which they are experiencing difficulty. The supervisor, using the group, works with the presenting supervisee in such a way as to enable him to resolve the ongoing impasse with his patient. The more experienced the supervisee, the more likely are his problems rooted in a countertransference resistance than in technical ignorance. The second level is the process level. The group supervisor is alert to ongoing tensions that might be building up within the group and interfering with the work of supervision. He works with the group members' resistance to verbalizing whatever latent or withheld thoughts and feelings they might be having in response to each other, the leader, or the supervisory situation. Following the resolution of such resistances, the group is enabled to bring their intellectual and emotional resources more fully to bear on the task of supervision. The group supervisor's method of dealing with group resistances constitutes a paradigm that seems to become internalized and carried over to the supervisees' work with their patients.

In the process of conducting group supervision the supervisor gets feedback that is rarely forthcoming in the one-to-one tutorial situation. From such feedback I have learned the following:

Most standard supervisory interventions that are spontaneously offered to the presenting supervisees, either by myself or by others, are likely to be experienced as unhelpful or critical, making the supervisee feel anxious, wrong, and inadequate, thereby increasing his reluctance to present cases in the group. In effect this means that the "supervisory impulse," if acted upon without being internally processed for its possible impact on the other, is, more likely than not, to be unresponsive to the supervisee's need.

I also learned that the more I follow the practice of explaining and formulating whatever it is that I might feel like formulating and explaining, the more I will be admired by the group members yet the worse they will feel about themselves. The connection between my behavior and the supervisees' reactions is not usually immediately apparent either to myself or to them. They might report during the group session that they are feeling depressed, or they might later report that they left the session feeling depressed, or during a given session members might report that they feel some resistance to being in the group that day. It is through investigating such symptomatic negative reactions that the latent connection becomes clear.

A MODIFIED SUPERVISORY APPROACH

Such is the power of the reverse parallel process that it applies as well to the unconscious transmission of the supervisor's positive impact to the treatment situation. More than this, the supervisory process can profoundly influence such processes of internalization as the assimilation of enduring therapeutic values and enduring identifications with the supervisor. For this reason I have become increasingly interested in understanding how the supervisory relationship might be conducted so that the supervisor's treatment of the supervisee can be internalized with good effect.

In considering how my supervisory approach has changed in response to the above considerations, I conclude that there are two main revisions. One is that I make a conscious effort to focus no less of my interest and attention on the supervisee than on his work with his patient. This means that I attempt to take full account of his feelings and reactions vis-à-vis both the supervisory and treatment situations. The other revision is the application to the supervisory relationship of the practice that I have termed, following Sullivan (1940), active-participant-observation (Epstein 1982).

This practice requires the supervisor to be consistently alert to the impact of his personality style, his interventions, and of the entire supervisory process on the supervisee. It requires him to be ready at all times to investigate this impact and to enable the supervisee to put his feelings and reactions into words with a minimal accompanying sense of risk. The management of the supervisee's gradient of anxiety in working with his resistances, both to the supervisory process and to the therapeutic interaction, becomes as important in the supervisor's conduct of the supervisory inter-action as is the management of the patient's gradient of anxiety in the therapist's conduct of the therapeutic interaction. The prac-tice of participant-observation models is an interactional process that becomes internalized by the supervisee and is carried over to his work with his patients.

Now I would like to move from the general to the specific.

In applying participant-observation to a new supervisory rela-tionship, I am, to begin with, less focused on how I treat the super-visee than I am on studying his reactions to my interventions. As I learn how he is affected, I adjust my communications accordingly. I take notice, for instance, of his facial expressions and body lan-guage. I notice behaviors that signify anxiety such as nail biting or fidgeting. One supervisee would signal a heightening of anxiety by frantic note-taking. Should I comment that I seem to be mak-ing the supervisee uncomfortable, I am alert to whether my com-ment enables him to elaborate his thoughts and feelings vis-à-vis his experience of the supervision or whether he becomes more defensive or self-conscious. I ask myself such questions as: Should I back off? Should I ask a minimum number of questions—and only out of a need for clarification? Should I wait until the supervisee contacts me or should I respond to the signs he may be giving of needing something from me?

I operate on the assumption that persisting negative behav-iors, such as lateness or missing sessions, are resistances signifying negative reactions to the supervision. I might ask, "What is there about the way I am conducting this supervision that might be making you less eager to get here?" Should the supervisee fail to carry out agreed upon interventions, I would ask him what he felt was wrong with the intervention or the supervision. It may turn out that his failure to intervene effectively is due to intense negative countertransference reactions toward the patient which he needs help in contacting and putting into words. He may, for instance, discover that unwittingly he has been withholding potentially helpful interventions because of unformulated hateful thoughts and feelings toward a patient who has been tormenting him.

More often than not, when a patient is going into a decline, it is due to the therapist's failure to enable the patient to put ongoing, selectively inattended negative feelings about the therapist and the therapy into words. This usually requires the supervisor to resolve the supervisee's resistance to receiving and accepting such feelings from his patient. [This is most effectively done by, first, resolving the supervisee's resistance to contacting and expressing any feelings of disappointment and dissatisfaction he might be having vis-à-vis the supervision and the supervisor.] An effective approach to resolving this resistance is to suggest to the supervisee that since the patient is continuing to get worse, there must be something wrong with the supervision and that the supervisee's help is needed in discovering what it is that is wrong. If the supervisor can overcome his own resistance to accepting, as a simple matter of fact, that the supervision is failing the supervisee, he will be in a good position to initiate a process that results in the therapist helping the patient contact and communicate feelings of being failed by the therapist—as the patient was by his parents—thereby transforming a passive-aggressive, treatment-destructive, negative therapeutic reaction into an open and direct expression of dissatisfaction and disappointment.

I favor whenever possible the use of what Spotnitz (1969) has termed, "object-oriented questions" as contrasted with "ego-oriented questions." These questions direct the supervisee's attention to the faults of the other, to myself or to the patient, rather than to his own faults. This technique might appear to further the supervisee's tendency to externalize responsibility for his own contribution to the failure of the supervision or of the treatment situation. Actually it has the opposite effect. Object-oriented questions establish an atmosphere in which the supervisee becomes increasingly free, with a minimal sense of risk, to contact and directly communicate all of his feelings about both the supervision and his patient. The supervisee's experience of having his negative thoughts and feel-

ings matter-of-factly received and accepted by the supervisor becomes transmuted into a greater capability for identifying, articu-
lating, and tolerating his own faults and errors.

When the supervisee reports interventions that strike me as
incorrect or ill-timed, I work hard to stifle my impulse to offer
correction immediately. I try to wait until there is some evidence
either that the intervention didn't take or that it has resulted in a
negative therapeutic reaction. At that point I might ask the supervisee what he was attempting to accomplish with the intervention.
Did he think his purpose was accomplished? If not, why not? In
responding to this sequence of questions, the supervisee may contact selectively inattended anxiety aroused by something in the
therapeutic interaction.

> As an example of this, a supervisee recently reported that she
> reminded her patient that the patient had been treated badly
> by her brothers in the past. Because this intervention not only
> seemed to be irrelevant, but also turned out to be disruptive
> to the flow of the session, I asked the supervisee what she had
> in mind in making this intervention. In response to my inquiry
> the supervisee recalled that she was beginning to feel anxious
> at that moment in the session. This was in response to her sense
> that the patient was running out of material. She realized that
> she wanted to keep the patient talking in order to prevent her
> from reaching the point where she would begin to complain
> about therapy and question its usefulness. The intervention,
> in other words, was unwittingly designed to keep things go-
> ing in order to enable the therapist to avoid experiencing the
> feeling of being a bad or no-good therapist.

As a way of furthering the aim of enabling the supervisee to
internalize the practice of participant observation, I am in favor
of his making whatever interventions he may be inclined to make
followed by a non-critical study of their positive or negative effects.

I place a great emphasis on working with the supervisee's countertransference reactions. This is especially important in supervising situations involving borderline and psychotic patients. I am referring to feelings of inadequacy, impotence, helplessness, stupidity, confusion, frustration, anger, hate, sadism, contempt, disgust, punitive feelings, wishing the patient dead, sexual feelings, and so forth. Supervisees will feel themselves to be gravely at fault for having such feelings and desires and are likely to be ashamed of themselves if they have been indoctrinated with the concept that analytic neutrality means emotional neutrality (Reich 1951, 1960). Emotional neutrality is a myth, and I believe that it may be dangerous for a patient if his therapist actually assumes that he can operate from a position of emotional neutrality.

When strong countertransference feelings are aroused in response to the powerful primitive projective processes of borderline and psychotic patients, it will be difficult and, at times, impossible to prevent such feelings from seeping either into the therapist's communications or into his way of being with his patient. The best way the analyst can protect his patient from the noxious effects of negative countertransference feelings is to begin by fully owning and confronting such feelings.

Supervisees, more often than not, conclude from the very fact of having intense emotional reactions to their patients that this signifies they are doing bad therapy. Frequently, in such a context, when asked if a patient is doing badly, the supervisee may say, matter of factly, that the patient is doing well—as if the patient's progress were something apart from, and having no connection with, this "bad therapy" of which the therapist presumes himself to be guilty. Usually the supervisee will resist any effort to address the issue of how or why it might be possible for the patient to be doing well in such a negative emotional context. He may be incapable of thinking seriously about such questions until he is enabled to accept all of his feelings and adopt a relaxed and tolerant attitude toward them.

I attempt to accomplish this by asking such questions as, "What's wrong with hating the patient?," "Wishing him dead?," "Wanting to have sex with the patient?," and so on. If the supervisee complains that he feels helpless or impotent I would ask, "How does the patient prefer you to feel?" or "Does the patient prefer you to feel like a good-competent analyst or like a bad-incompetent one?"

I generally compare feelings to the weather. There is nothing you can do about a bad-weather system except to wait for it to pass through the area.

I work to enable the supervisee ultimately to value his feelings, whatever they may be, and to understand that in owning and containing them, rather than acting on them, he will be performing an essential, maturationally corrective function for his more disturbed patients. He will be, in effect, breaching a lifelong, compulsively repetitious, interpersonal vicious cycle of projection and counterprojection which has kept such patients fixated in their state of developmental arrest.

Once the supervisee learns to value the feelings that are aroused in the therapeutic interaction, he will be in a better position to understand something about their meaning and function in the context of ongoing therapeutic interaction and to formulate what he might do with such feelings in order to benefit his patient. Should he contain them and protect his patient from them, should he convey them in tones of speech? Should he use them to formulate questions or interpretations?

I shall illustrate this approach by presenting three clinical vignettes.

VIGNETTE 1

A supervisee, with considerable discomfort, presented a male patient whom he was treating. He described his own experience in the treatment as alternating between "being lost and being found." Occasionally there were moments or possibly a whole session in which he felt he understood the patient and felt comfortable in interacting with him. For the most part, however, he felt lost, confused, stupid, and very inadequate.

He made this presentation at a moment of crisis. The patient had just informed him that he was quitting therapy because he had become addicted to cocaine. He had concealed this addiction throughout the course of the treatment. He had just applied to a drug program, but this was not why he wanted to leave therapy. He wanted to leave therapy because he felt he had ruined it. He had agreed to come back for another session to discuss the matter further. The therapist said he had no idea what to do with this patient, and he felt like a total failure.

I asked the therapist if he thought there might be some way his feelings were related to the patient's feelings. The therapist said yes and elaborated on how the patient probably felt lost, confused, like a failure but that he covered this up with a macho manner. The supervisee also suspected that the patient needed to use cocaine in order to enable him to maintain this macho exterior and to contain himself, because he was probably terrified of falling apart or going crazy.

The supervisee remembered that the patient grew up in a household dominated by a macho father who often lost control and went into terrifying rages. In reflecting on the way the patient behaved in the sessions with him, he realized that there were many cues that the patient was internally very agitated. He would, for instance, hit himself very hard on the knee for emphasis while talking.

After very little discussion the supervisee was able to understand that the patient probably needed his therapist to contain and ride out the emotional turbulence induced by the therapeutic interaction. The supervisee found himself able to do this the next time that he was with the patient, and he reported that it had an immediate soothing effect.

In this example the therapist's countertransference resistance, or more accurately, his resistance to his countertransference, was mainly based on a lack of understanding as to how he might use this experience to understand the therapeutic interaction and gain control of it. Once he reached this understanding, he was able to implement it successfully, indicating the relative absence of subjective factors that might have interfered with his capability of using such understanding.

VIGNETTE 2

This vignette involves a therapist who was quite capable of tolerating her induced feelings and was quite sophisticated in understanding how they might be used therapeutically. In the situation presented for supervision, however, subjective factors had to be dealt with before she could be relieved of her countertransference resistance and be enabled to use the countertransference experience to work effectively with this therapeutic situation. The therapist presented the situation in two stages. It involved a couple, consisting of her primary patient and her patient's husband. The patient married this man after two years of therapy, knowing that he was very immature and a heavy cocaine user. The marriage soon began to deteriorate. Each partner felt abused and misunderstood and uncared for by the other. The husband was referred by the supervisee to a number of competent therapists, all of whom he rejected. He agreed to attend couple sessions, but only with the supervisee.

Under pressure from the wife, the supervisee began couple sessions. They turned out to be chaotic. Both husband and wife persistently made destructive communications to each other. The husband frequently would disrupt the session by walking out.

The supervisee felt both hopeless and helpless. In supervision she began to feel all the more so by the fact that she had already tried almost every intervention that I had suggested.

The supervisee was asked how she would feel if she were able to stop seeing the couple. She said she would feel very relieved.

She was then asked if there was any reason why she should not inform the couple that she was discontinuing couple sessions because she found herself incapable of getting them to behave themselves and to communicate constructively. The supervisee found this suggestion agreeable, and she decided to follow it. She decided to see the husband individually as well as the wife. She was afraid of the consequences for the marriage should she abandon him totally. Although she found his behavior intolerable in the couple sessions, she now found him more tolerable, sometimes even likeable, in the individual sessions.

In the next supervisory session, she reported that while she continued to feel relieved at not having to suffer through conjoint sessions, she still felt greatly stressed and under a great deal of pressure to help these people, to save their marriage. She felt hopeless about succeeding. She was also very afraid of the husband's potential violence to his wife.

She was helped in supervision to elaborate her hateful feelings toward both these patients, to the husband for being what she called an infantile creep, and to the wife for marrying him and messing up the good work that she was doing before the marriage. The therapist was then asked why she found it necessary to save this marriage? Why not let the marriage break up? She might then have the patient back in treatment by herself, like in the good-old-days. In response to this question, the therapist had the recognition that vis-à-vis this couple she found herself in the same terrible emotional situation that she experienced growing up in her family. Her younger brother, she said, almost from the time he was born, was a source of great trouble and conflict within the family. He was constantly upsetting her parents, and they were incapable of coping with him. It was her role to be the family peacemaker from the time she was a small child. She was frequently terrified that her family would break up and often felt helpless and hopeless. She realized that there were many times that she hated her brother and wished that she could get rid of him so that peace and harmony could be restored to her family life.

The supervisee was asked if she were able to give up the project of trying to save the marriage. She was also asked if, whenever she felt impotent in response to pressure from either the wife or the husband to improve the marriage, she would be able, matter-of-factly, to communicate such feelings. The supervisee said that she found these suggestions agreeable and that she now understood that the couple, in all likelihood, had made her the depository of all mature concern and responsibility for making their marriage work. It was as if they had split off and externalized their unwanted superego and activated it in the therapist. This freed them of all internal conflict and enabled them to give full range to their infantile destructive impulses, which included defeating her every effort to help them. In succumbing to the pressure to save their marriage, the therapist understood that she was unwittingly preventing the couple from feeling any internal pressure to control their behavior toward each other.

VIGNETTE 3

A supervisee reported that he was feeling very frustrated and abused by a female patient. She had bounced two checks and had not, as yet, made good on them. In addition, she refused to cooperate in changing her appointment time, which had been given to her at the start of the summer with the understanding that it was temporary and that she was expected to resume her regular appointments in September. The current schedule was preventing the supervisee from attending supervisory sessions on time. It was now December and the patient continued to refuse to cooperate.

I asked the supervisee, "Why can't you tell the patient that you will discontinue treatment with her until she pays her bill? And why can't you tell her that you can no longer see her until she is ready and willing to change her appointment time as she originally agreed?" The supervisee responded as follows, "She starts to argue with me and it becomes too difficult. I get frustrated and I begin to feel sadistic. When I get angry the patient gets terribly upset and I feel like a terrible person. I can't stand these feelings."

I commented that the supervisee seemed capable with other patients of setting limits and, if necessary, tolerating bad feelings.

He said there was something else. There was the matter of the referral source. The referral source is a senior colleague. The patient was a nurse who worked in the same hospital as the referral source. The supervisee was afraid to lose both the respect of the referral source and future referrals.

I asked the supervisee, "Why would the referral source lose respect for you and not send you any more patients?"

He responded, "This patient will complain that I'm mercenary and that I'm sadistic and that I mistreat her. She'll ruin my reputation."

At this point I was feeling a rising frustration and some annoyance, and I recognized that I was impotent to help the supervisee overcome his resistance to setting some limits that would stop his patient from torturing and bullying him. I also recognized that something of a parallel process was being created with me. I opted not to communicate my understanding of this situation to the supervisee because I had no confidence that he would experience it as helpful. I thought that at best he might find such information mildly interesting. At worst, I expected that he would feel criticized and feel worse about himself for unwittingly inducing this parallel process. I did not think that aggravating his bad feelings would enable him to function more effectively with his patient.

I decided, instead, to extricate myself from the parallel process by matter-of-factly and comfortably signifying my acceptance of my failure to have any direct influence on him. By disengaging myself in this way, I hoped that I might indirectly enable the supervisee to take appropriate action with his patient. I said the following: "Since you are unwilling to upset the patient because you can't stand feeling like a bad person and since you can't take a chance on having the patient ruin your reputation and your referral source, the situation seems helpless to me. I can see no alternative, for the time being, to your continuing to be abused and frustrated by this patient."

The supervisee later reported that in the next session with his patient he informed her that he was discontinuing further sessions until she paid him what she owed him and until she agreed to come at an alternative time. The patient, not at all upset, said that it made sense to her that therapy sessions should be discontinued until she was able to catch up financially. She said that she would pay her bill as soon as possible so that she could resume her sessions. The supervisee said he was very satisfied with this solution and he was confident that the patient would soon be returning to treatment at a more agreeable appointment time.

CONCLUSION

I would summarize the main features that differentiate the approach put forth in this chapter from the traditional tutorial method as follows.

The supervisor works to enable the supervisee to contact and put into words, with a minimal accompanying sense of risk, the widest possible range of negative thoughts and feelings vis-à-vis the supervisor, the supervision, and his patient. In this way the development of tacit collusion between supervisor and supervisee to ignore indications of the supervisor's possible negative impact, either on the supervisee or on his work with the patient under supervision, is limited, and the supervisee is helped to protect his patient from toxic countertransference feelings.

The supervisor's attentiveness to the supervisee's needs and feelings, along with his practice of active participant-observation, constitute a paradigm of interpersonal relatedness that the supervisee may be expected to internalize and carry over to his work with his patients with good effect. The relational aspect of this supervisory approach, then, is no less, and possibly more, a fundamental source of learning than are the more straightforward didactic communications of the supervisor.

I would expect that this model of supervision is less compatible than is the traditional tutorial model with the aims and practices of the training committees of most psychoanalytic institutes. The primary concern of training committees is, typically, to oversee and evaluate the candidate's assimilation of supervision. Its aim is to keep itself and the supervisee informed about those of his limitations which may be retarding his progress toward becoming a competent enough analyst to be certified as such and graduated by the institute. It is generally considered to be the supervisee's responsibility to correct his deficiencies.

In the model put forth in this chapter, the supervisor monitors and evaluates the supervisee's assimilation of supervision, but with a different purpose: namely, to ascertain the effectiveness of his own conduct of the supervisory relationship. If he notes that the supervision is not taking, before ascribing fault to the supervisee, the supervisor assumes responsibility for investigating and determining how his conduct of the supervision might be contributing to the supervisee's difficulties. He then attempts to revise his approach accordingly.

Thus there is no more pressure placed on the supervisee to progress in the supervision than would be placed on a patient in analysis. Here the view taken of progress is essentially a maturational one. Because of this it might be argued that treating the supervisee in this way implies some disrespect for him as a responsible adult. I can only say that in my experience this approach is generally successful in[facilitating steady progress toward both psychoanalytic competence and mature professionalism] In this interpersonal context, the supervisee seems to experience himself as more consistently respected as an adult than in the more authoritarian tutorial relationship. In the latter, because he receives a steady flow of communications informing him about his errors and faults, he often finds himself in the emotional position of a bad and deficient child.

The traditional method of psychoanalytic training and supervision, despite its authoritarian tilt, has worked well enough to achieve its main aim, which is to graduate competent analysts. Because it works and because it is subject neither to internal nor external pressure to change, like any ongoing system, it is likely to resist change. For this reason a more maturationally oriented approach can be more freely practiced outside of the setting of formal psychoanalytic training.

Psychoanalytic understanding, however, despite the fact that it continues to be both essentially conservative and highly politicized, seems to be inexorably progressive. New concepts of theory and practice that prove themselves valid seem to be gradually assimilated, in one way or another—sometimes after being discovered anew—into various schools of psychoanalytic thought. I would expect that the ideas put forth in this paper on the supervisory practice will also, to the extent that they are valid, be gradually integrated with the traditional model to soften its evaluative emphasis and to correct its authoritarian tilt.

REFERENCES

Doehrman, M. J. G. (1976). Parallel processes in supervision and psychotherapy. *Bulletin of the Menninger Clinic* 40:3–104.

Epstein, L. (1982). Adapting to the patient's therapeutic need in the psychoanalytic situation. *Contemporary Psychoanalysis* 18:190–217.

Erikson, E. H. (1964). *Insight and Responsibility.* New York: Norton.

Fiscalini, J. (1985). On supervisory parataxis and dialogue. *Contemporary Psychoanalysis* 21:591–608.

Freud, S. (1905). A case of hysteria. *Standard Edition* 7:3–122.

Gediman, H. K., and Wolkenfeld, F. (1980). The parallelism phenomenon in psychoanalysis: its reconsideration as a triadic system. *Psychoanalytic Quarterly* 49:234–255.

Lesser, R. M. (1983). Supervision: illusions, anxieties, and questions. *Contemporary Psychoanalysis* 19:120–129.

Reich, A. (1951). On countertransference. *International Journal of Psycho-Analysis* 32:25–31.

————. (1960). Further remarks on countertransference. *International Journal of Psycho-Analysis* 41:389–395.

Searles, H. F. (1962). Problems of psychoanalytic supervision. In *Collected Papers on Schizophrenia and Related Subjects*, pp. 584–604. New York: International Universities Press.

Spotnitz, H. (1969). *Modern Psychoanalysis of the Schizophrenic Patient.* New York: Grune & Stratton.

Stern, D. B. (1983). Unformulated experience. *Contemporary Psychoanalysis* 19:71–99.

Sullivan, H. S. (1940). *Conceptions of Modern Psychiatry.* New York: Norton.

11

The Use of the Countertransference in Supervision

WINSLOW HUNT

Goin and Kline (1976), in a recent study, have shown that the majority of psychotherapy supervisors either ignore completely the countertransference emotions of their supervisees or else approach them with extreme circumspection. These supervisors adopt this almost phobic attitude toward the countertransference out of a concern that they may, from their position of authority, inappropriately intrude into the personality and inner life of the student-therapist, or they fear that supervision may turn into psychotherapy. A minority of supervisors, however, do routinely use the countertransference of the student in supervision in a way that is helpful for the student, and no difficulties arise. For most supervisors the student's countertransference seems to be a Pandora's box they fear to open, while others can rush in where angels fear to tread and, mysteriously, the feared consequences never materialize. After demonstrating that this is the case, Goin and Kline do not go on to explain how one can and should use countertransference data in supervision. The purpose of this chapter is to do just that: to offer guidelines for utilizing the counter-transference in supervision and to describe the rationale behind these suggestions.

In this chapter, countertransference is defined as whatever the therapist feels in relation to his patient, without implying anything about the origins of those feelings. Upon analysis, each counter-transference experience will be found to be both a response to the patient and a reflection of the therapist's personality. The relative importance of each component will vary from instance to instance, but also will depend upon the purpose for which the analysis is undertaken.

It is important to examine the student's countertransference in supervision, and it is possible to do so in a way that is helpful to the student's learning, that in no way violates his privacy, and that engages him in psychotherapy only in the sense that it encourages an ongoing, self-analytic process that should in any case be a continuing part of a therapist's life. The rest of this chapter will describe and illustrate the general principles of this approach to supervision.

Supervisors who do not deal with the student's countertrans-ference might justify their method with the argument that coun-tertransference is not a significant part of psychotherapy—all that counts is the cognitive grasp of the patient's psychodynamics and of therapeutic technique. I have never heard this argument given nor is it to be found in the literature. Psychiatrists who are hesi-tant to approach the countertransference experience of their supervisees may in their own work give considerable attention and weight to their feelings about the patient.

Another view, and one that is raised in this connection, is that countertransference, while admittedly important, derives centrally from the therapist's own neurotic conflicts. This goes to the heart of the problem and no doubt explains the reluctance of most super-visors to enter this area. To clarify this issue, let us imagine a psy-chiatric resident who has an upsetting experience with a patient. Let us suppose that he has been surprised and disturbed by the intensity of the apparent inappropriateness of his feelings toward his patient. Luckily, he has both a supervisor and an analyst with whom he can talk it over. In supervision, they explore the incident in an outward direction, using the resident's emotional reaction as the starting point. What did the patient do that made him react that way? What could the patient's motives have been? How does that connect with the ongoing process of therapy? With the patient's childhood? And so on. When the resident leaves he will know more about his patient.

With his analyst he again describes the same incident and they explore it in an inward direction. What memories does this stir up? What long-standing wishes, impulses, and fears does this contact with the patient mobilize? How does this connect with the resident's own transference, his current life, the past? When he leaves he will know more about himself. Although both supervisor and analyst have started with the same experience their studies have explored differing spaces. Neither has trespassed on the other's territory nor is the resident at all confused about their respective roles.

In supervision, our purpose is to increase the student's understanding of the patient and of the treatment process. If he learns more about himself, and he usually does, that is frosting on the cake, not our central goal. The supervisor should maintain a mental set which always asks "What does this tell us about the patient?"

When a therapist comes to supervision, the best place to start is to give him a chance to express his feelings toward the patient and the progress of the treatment. Therapists often arrive carrying a considerable load of unresolved emotion derived from the impact of the patient and they need a chance to express it and have it accepted. No one does their best thinking if they are jammed up with unventilated affects. Starting with the therapist's feelings about the patient usually leads one to the central current problem more directly than would a chronological account.

The student-therapist often tries to dismiss his feelings by relating them to something in his personal life, a fact that probably plays a role in the reluctance of supervisors to pursue the matter. This maneuver, however, is usually defensive and escapist, an unconscious attempt to avoid facing something in the relationship with the patient. For instance, the therapist may attribute his irritability in the therapy session to having been on call the night before, or a tiff with his wife at breakfast, thereby overlooking the fact that the patient has been, in some covert way, attacking him. He unconsciously knows that if he perceives the covert hostility and interprets it, he will promptly be confronted with that hostility in less covert forms. However useful that may be in the long run, it may be frightening and unpleasant to endure in the short run. The supervisor can keep the therapy on course by not accepting the personal connection as the whole story, but by insisting that, however valid this aspect of the situation may be, the therapist's emotions in the session are in some way responsive to the patient.

It is quite different when, late in the supervisory session, after the interaction with the patient has been clarified, the student tries to enlarge an insight already achieved by connecting it with matters in his personal life, or in his work with other patients. This is usually a constructive process of integrating and working through a piece of learning. The supervisor can at this point be most helpful, and keep his function sharply delineated by being an accepting audience for a bit of self-analysis, and nothing more. Once the supervisor has created a climate in which self-revelation on the part of the therapist is welcomed, then the inner emotional part of the therapist's interaction with the patient comes out easily and is included naturally in the ongoing story.

The supervisor's attitude toward the countertransference can create a kind of self-fulfilling prophecy. If the supervisor believes that a reported emotional reaction to the patient means neurotic conflict in the therapist, and pursues the matter in that sense, he will, if the student cooperates, come up with data to support his original opinion. This has to do with the "overdetermination" of every experience described earlier. Usually the student will not cooperate in such a project, and rightly so, since he has not entered into any contract with the supervisor which would justify such investigation of his personal life.

Any implication that certain emotional reactions to the patient are wrong or inappropriate places the therapist in a particularly difficult position. Emotional reactions to the patient are continuous and universal. How much a therapist notices this fact depends only on how much he directs his attention to this penumbra of awareness. If a student is led, however subtly, to feel that some of these reactions are bad, he can only try to suppress awareness of them, or acknowledge their existence and feel deficient and/or guilty, none of which is conducive to growth and learning.

If the supervisor feels that the ongoing emotional response to the patient is unimportant or off-limits, then he will busy himself with other things, details of the patient's history or symptomatology, near-to-verbatim reporting of sessions, and so on. The student will get the message that his feelings about the patient are not relevant and will not report them. The supervisor will learn nothing of all the therapist's fantasies, dreams, and impulses that involve the patient and may therefore continue in his belief that such matters are nonexistent, trivial, or irrelevant.

For example, an analytic candidate was attempting, under supervision, to do insight psychotherapy with a certain young man. His supervisor was unhappy with his performance and said, "Doctor, you have a countertransference problem here. Take it up with your analyst." Such an approach is quite unhelpful and puts the student in a difficult position.

First, he cannot meaningfully, by conscious resolution alone, put an item on the agenda of his own psychotherapy. More important, by dismissing a countertransference reaction, by declaring it persona non grata in the supervisory session, the supervisor deprives himself and his student of important information about the patient and the treatment process.

In this particular case, what bothered the supervisor was that the candidate was not "analytic" enough. He continually failed to maintain the proper distance, silence, and passivity. Despite his best efforts he was too supportive and active. Eventually he did learn to perform according to the model his supervisor had in mind, whereupon the patient gradually but impressively became psychotic. In retrospect it is clear that the therapist's "countertransference problem" was (among other things) a response to certain traits in the patient, such as his very high anxiety level and subtle paranoid trends. Had this been attended to earlier, a more appropriate treatment might have been instituted and both patient and therapist spared some unpleasant moments.

Before illustrating this approach to utilizing countertransference data in psychotherapy supervision, and to make the illustrations more understandable, it is necessary to summarize briefly some of what we know about the psychodynamics of the supervisory process. The literature on countertransference itself is beyond the scope of this paper and has in any case been recently summarized by Sandler and colleagues (1970). Heinrich Racker (1953, 1957), the first author to systematically formulate the dynamics of countertransference, also was the first to advocate giving priority to its examination in supervision. Searles (1955) and Arlow (1963) noticed that the student does to the supervisor what the patient has done to him. In particular, it is those aspects of the patient's impact on him that the student-therapist cannot be conscious of, cannot articulate, and cannot cope with, that are acted out in relation to the supervisor. It follows from this that what the supervisor feels toward his student, and what he observes of the student's behavior towards him, is full of clues about the interaction between patient and therapist. Ekstein and Wallerstein (1958) emphasized the importance to all concerned—patient, therapist, and supervisor— of the treatment setting and of their relationship to the administration of the clinic or hospital. They also note that the student-therapist's personality affects his relationship to his patient and to his supervisor in characteristic and similar ways. Doehrman (1976) describes a process which is the converse of that noted by Searles and Arlow. Students develop quite intense transferences toward their supervisors and act out, in their treatment of the patient, impulses and affects arising from this source. In summary, the chain of individuals, patient-therapist-supervisor, constitutes a single system and significant affective constellations move with ease along it in both directions.

The following supervisory anecdotes are chosen to illustrate how, in a wide variety of situations, a focus on the countertransference emotions can lead to insights which may open an impasse in the treatment or at least deepen the understanding of the patient and/or the therapeutic process.

ILLUSTRATIVE VIGNETTES

Case 1

The resident brought up the case of a woman teacher with a moderate depression whose life situation and preoccupations centered around obtaining compensation for an injury suffered about fifteen months previously. She brought out her difficulties with the many agencies and courts involved, telling how much she felt mistreated and suspected of malingering. She had been raised in a refined, middle-class home and was not prepared for dealing with the roughness of life in the cold, hard world. Both Dr. B. and I realized that her complaint that various officials felt she was malingering was an indirect reproach against the therapist, whom she suspected of the same attitude. I asked Dr. B. whether her perception was correct—did he in his heart really feel she was malingering. The resident did not like the question and made it clear that he did not think that there was any conscious malingering on her part. However, the question of whether she was unconsciously using or overusing her injury was unresolved in his mind. He noted that she still claimed some difficulty concentrating—even fifteen months afterwards—which could be considered as part of an organic postconcussion syndrome. However, that was a "soft" sign and in fact the whole neurological picture had been one of soft signs. Her previous life situation had been unhappy; she was unmarried, and while she enjoyed her work with students, she was always in some difficulty with the school authorities. She might be eager to seize on a chance to get out of a difficult situation. The sum she might win was equal to several years' salary. On the other hand, her previous life showed nothing psychopathic in it. I had the impression that he felt like a judge in a courtroom weighing the evidence pro and con. When this was pointed out, the resident at once realized that this was how he felt, and that he experienced it as a burdensome obligation from which he wanted to free himself. He reexamined the patient's way of relating to him and realized that she had presented herself in such a way as to implicitly ask whether what she was doing was honest and fair. The resident realized that the patient herself must be experiencing a great deal of inner conflict, greed versus guilt, over whether or not she has a just case, and probably accuses herself of being a malingerer.

Subsequent sessions with the patient confirmed that the therapist's mental state—sifting the evidence—did in fact reflect the patient's doubt and guilt. Unfortunately these sessions also revealed that the patient had never really agreed to a self-exploratory process and was not willing to pursue it.

Case 2

In the previous supervisory session (concerned with another patient), I had emphasized the importance of monitoring the patient's progress, both behavior changes over months and years of treatment and the dynamic changes within each session. At the beginning of this next session, the resident said he felt quite guilty about the patient he would present because there had been little progress and he had allowed the therapy to drift.

The patient was a working married woman in her twenties. She had begun treatment two years earlier because of marital difficulties and dissatisfaction with life. She was the older of two daughters of the only doctor in a small town, which made her family part of the local aristocracy. Her mother had married up into this status and enjoyed it, but insecurely. Her parents wanted the patient to grow up and become part of "society." Her younger sister had gross emotional troubles and had gotten most of the parents' attention, which the patient resented. The patient did not really object to the way of life her parents had in mind for her, but out of resentment at their favoring her sister, she had unconsciously determined to frustrate their ambitions for her. During her adolescence, she had shown unmistakable signs of becoming a drop-out, causing her parvenu mother concern and fears of social slippage.

In presenting the history of the patient's treatment thus far, the resident described in passing her considerable improvement in work and social relations, but attached no importance to it. Instead he emphasized his frustration at what he felt was a stagnated treatment and his guilt at having allowed it to go on so long. My mini-lecture the week before on therapeutic progress had so mobilized this guilt over her supposed lack of progress that he had set her a deadline for ending the treatment in a desperate hope of somehow blowing up the logjam.

When I noted the disparity between her actual progress during the two years of therapy and his profound discouragement, he allowed that his feelings might have something to do with her way of presenting herself. He recalled that at scattered times she had said that she knew he wanted to change her in various ways and that it would give him a "real ego trip" if he were able to do so. She had also said that he was already rich in pleasing traits of character and in satisfactions in life and hinted her determination not to "give to those as have too much before." The fact that the patient could so clearly articulate the motive behind her negative therapeutic stance (Rivière 1936) strengthened my opinion that there was more going right with the treatment than the therapist appreciated. The resident recalled more evidence that she was stubbornly refusing to let him derive any satisfaction from her progress.

But he continued in his anxiety for her—she was wasting her life, in that she was not enjoying her successes at work or her life with her husband, and he felt powerless to change this. I speculated that her mother might have felt just this way when the patient was threatening downward mobility. The therapist experienced this as a liberating "Aha!" insight which got him at once unhooked from the patient and her world. He spent the rest of the supervisory session elaborating on his previously unconscious identification with the mother and the ways in which she had induced this in him.

When he returned to the patient he rescinded the deadline, said that he felt he had been drawn into feeling and behaving like her mother, and continued to interpret the patient's transference in this sense. She responded with more memories of her own parents' demanding control and her own fears that she would never find her own true self and way, but only live out their plans for her.

Case 3

This case was presented by a female psychiatric resident at two sessions of a seminar devoted to countertransference problems. She felt that the patient was too special to her and in addition was troubled by a need to do "something more" for him, though she did not know what that "something more" might be.

The patient was a man in his late twenties who had contracted polio at one year of age. The disease had left him largely crippled from the waist down. He was unable to get about except in a wheel-chair. He was bright and articulate, with considerable education, but had been in trouble due to defiant behavior in school and college. There had been several suicide attempts, one of which resulted in psychiatric hospitalization eighteen months earlier. For reasons not clear to her the resident had chosen him to treat from among other patients admitted at the same time.

Prior to admission he had had several close relationships with women. Dr. A. knew little about these relationships. She also did not know what sexual functions were intact in the patient. This ignorance contrasted with the generally well-organized and adequately detailed case presentation. When questioned, Dr. A. realized she had been afraid to investigate this area for fear it would be humiliating to the patient to have to confess his sexual inadequacy. Full normal sexuality was obviously impossible regardless of what actual genital functioning was intact. As soon as the matter was opened up she realized that to avoid this area was also a communication and might be viewed by the patient as indicating that she thought him a nonsexual and incomplete creature.

The treatment thus far had centered around the patient's feeling of entitlement and its many ramifications. The therapist and hospital staff refused to accept that his misfortunes entitled him to special treatment and they did not let him make an exception of himself on the ward. This approach had been effective in forcing the patient to bring to consciousness his enormous resentment at the unfairness of fate. At the present time he was, in various ways, expressing the feeling that his therapist did not care for him enough. Dr. A. felt that the patient was right in this regard, although she could not find any way in which she had in reality been an inadequate therapist.

My own associations went to the fairy tale, "The Frog Prince." When the princess is finally persuaded to let the ugly frog sleep on her pillow, an evil spell is broken and the frog turns into a handsome prince. I suggested that there might be some connection between her sense of guilt for not loving the patient enough and our ignorance about his sexual life. The resident then told how she had at times tried to imagine what sex with the patient would be like, but had always been unable to carry the fantasy through, partly because of her lack of knowledge about his sexual function, but even more by some feeling of horror toward the patient's crippled lower body. At this point our time was up.

At the next meeting, Dr. A. said that she felt that I had implied that she could never treat the patient effectively unless she were able in fantasy, or perhaps even in reality, to have a full sexual relationship with this man. I corrected this impression. This time (reminded of St. Francis, who slept with the leper and breathed into his mouth) I assured her I did not consider sainthood a necessary prerequisite to doing effective psychotherapy.

The group discussion picked up the theme, wondering whether Dr. A. believed that only if she made physical love to him, could the patient really accept himself, and then going on to wonder if the patient himself had this belief. Dr. A. reported data from interviews with the parents indicating that they never made up their minds whether to see their son as a potentially full human being, which would include his being a sexual person, or to see him as only a partial creature, a *forme fruste* of a human being. By now, we all thought that this must be the central issue for the patient, embodied in the concrete question: Could his therapist imagine sexual relations with him? Dr. A. felt that this was the question that both she and the patient had been circling but were afraid to broach. She then recalled incidents during the patient's hospital stay in which he had become quite involved with nurses or female patients. She had marveled at his ability to engage the attention of attractive women. These incidents had been seen heretofore as only a matter of the patient expecting special treatment, that is, to be allowed to transgress certain barriers. She now saw them in quite another aspect, as the patient's efforts to get her to consider that he might be a sexual creature and to reproach her for having assumed that for him a sexual life was out of the question. She also saw her idea that she should have sexual relations with him as a response, in concrete imagery, to his unspoken request that she confirm his (doubted) manhood and humanness.

DISCUSSION

Supervision that lets in the countertransference is the most helpful kind because it goes to the core of the therapist–patient relationship. It is also the most strenuous both for the supervisor and for the learning therapist. For the supervisor it is as difficult as the analysis of the transference in psychotherapy. Both situations require that he perceive the similarities between what is happening between himself and a person who is talking to him in the here and now and what that person is describing in the there and then. For the learning therapist it is difficult in that he is dealing with a situation in which his own emotions are highly engaged and in which there is usually some intrapsychic conflict.

For example, in the compensation case discussed above, the therapist was deeply involved in her identification with the patient's own conflicted indecision and self-judging. Grasping a new gestalt of the therapeutic interaction required strenuous shifts in her way of understanding and of feeling the situation. Such shifts are fatiguing and generally require some time for working through.

In therapy, if we do not understand the patient, it is often because the patient is not giving us that data which we need in order to understand him, and this usually reflects some problem in the therapeutic alliance. Similarly, when the supervisor does not understand her student's patient or therapy, it is often because there is some problem in the working alliance between supervisor and student-therapist that results in the supervisee not producing that fullness of material that would allow his supervisor to understand.

There are, of course, limiting cases in which the student's emotional problems are so great that the supervisor's attention is forced upon them and he must take some action, such as advising personal therapy or interrupting the treatment. In evaluating such situations it is often clarifying to know if the resident has a certain problem with all his patients or only with the one known to this supervisor.

Nothing in this chapter should be taken to imply that study of the student's countertransference should be the sole subject matter of supervision. Much of supervision is the straightforward teaching of facts and concepts that the resident simply needs to learn. In addition, much of the therapist's learning is based on modeling himself on the supervisor. The supervisor facilitates this

by, in imagination, placing himself in the therapist's role and telling what he observes and understands from that position and how
he would act were he the therapist. The supervisor should keep in
mind that there is usually no one right way to act in a given psychotherapeutic situation, and the student may be doing it well, even
if not quite the way the supervisor would handle things.

Early in the therapist's training he needs most urgently to learn
basics and as he masters these he can increasingly turn his attention to his countertransference reactions. With the beginner in
psychotherapy, it is his understanding of basic theory and technique that usually determines success or failure. With the more advanced therapist, it is deeper knowledge of psychodynamics and
the ability to use the countertransference which become the crucial factors. But even at the very beginning of his training, the student should see these emotional reactions not as a hindrance to
doing therapy, but as a helpful source of information.

CONCLUSION

The countertransference, the therapist's emotional reaction to the
patient at each point in time, should naturally and routinely be
part of the data under discussion in the supervisory session. The
countertransference is so important a part of the psychotherapeutic
process that to ignore it is to risk missing an important part, perhaps even the core, of what is happening in the treatment. The
countertransference can be utilized in supervision without risk of
intruding into the student-therapist's private life, or of turning
supervision into psychotherapy, if the supervisor maintains a mental set of readiness to seek the origins of the countertransference
emotions in the therapist's interaction with the patient. That these
countertransference emotions also have their connections with the
therapist's own neurotic conflicts is acknowledged and in no way
minimized, but this is left to one side as not germane to the goals
of supervision. The supervisor should always hold in mind the

question, "How can these emotional reactions of the therapist lead us to a deeper understanding of the patient, of the patient's current emotional situation, and of the therapeutic process?"

REFERENCES

Arlow, J. A. (1963). The supervisory situation. *Journal of the American Psychoanalytic Association* 11:576–594.

Doehrman, M. J. G. (1976). Parallel processes in supervision and psychotherapy. *Bulletin of the Menninger Clinic* 40:9–104.

Ekstein, R., and Wallerstein, R. S. (1958*). The Teaching and Learning of Psychotherapy*. New York: International Universities Press.

Goin, M. K., and Kline, F. (1976). Countertransference: a neglected subject in clinical supervision. *American Journal of Psychiatry* 133:41–44.

Racker, H. (1953). The countertransference neurosis. *International Journal of Psycho-Analysis* 34:313–325.

———. (1957). The meaning and uses of countertransference. *Psychoanalytic Quarterly* 2:303–357.

Rivière, J. (1936). A contribution to the analysis of the negative therapeutic reaction. *International Journal of Psycho-Analysis* 17:304–320.

Sandler, J., Holder, A., and Dare, C. (1970). Basic psychoanalytic concepts: IV. Countertransference. *British Journal of Psychiatry* 117:83–88.

Searles, H. F. (1955). The informational value of the supervisor's emotional experiences. *Psychiatry* 18:135–146.

12

Interpreting Transference in Supervision*
HOWARD E. GORMAN

INTRODUCTION

The two classical approaches to handling supervisee countertransference in psychoanalytic psychotherapy arose in the context of training supervisions early in the history of psychoanalysis. The approach promoted by the Viennese analysts viewed supervision as a strictly didactic procedure and insisted that countertransference be referred to the training analysis (Eitingon 1926). The other, favored by the Hungarian analysts, viewed supervision as an analytic procedure and as part of the training analysis. Supervisions were all to be conducted by the training analyst who would interpret supervisory countertransference as he would any other transference of the candidate (Kovacs 1936).

---

*The term *psychoanalytic psychotherapy*, used somewhat informally here, is meant to denote psychoanalysis or any psychotherapy in which psychoanalytic principles and conduct play a rigorous, governing role.

Both these approaches explicitly relied upon a training analysis to resolve countertransference. With the advent of more general, psychoanalytically informed psychotherapies that required no associated personal therapy, analytic therapists realized that the responsibility for addressing countertransference fell increasingly to the supervision itself. It might seem that this responsibility could be fulfilled if direct interpretation were allowed a place in supervision. However, the prevalent analytic opinion was, and continues to be, that directly interpreting countertransference in supervision is to be avoided as psychologically and pedagogically dangerous (Ekstein and Wallerstein 1972, Goin and Kline 1976). While generally acknowledging the close relation between supervision and psychotherapy, most analytic therapists continue to advocate that the supervisor "think like an analyst but not act like an analyst" (Schlesinger 1995, p. 192). Instead, methods were developed that viewed countertransference difficulties as learning problems and supervisors who became aware of such problems, either directly or via some form of supervisory parallel process, were to deal with them didactically (Goin and Kline 1976, Searles 1955). Supervisees for whom this process provided insufficient resolution were advised, but rarely required, to seek a personal therapy outside the training process.

This having been said, support for transference interpretation in supervision continues to have its adherents. Lester and Robertson (1995) find a useful place for supervisory interpretation of transferences and countertransferences in analytic training. In Gorman (1996), I re-examined the facilitating role of interpreting transference and countertransference in the supervision of any psychoanalytic psychotherapy. I contended that interpreting countertransference in the supervised case, and transference and countertransference in the supervision itself, has a legitimate role in promoting therapeutic progress and the growth of the supervisee as a therapist. I argued that *if this dual promotion is taken to be the purpose and focus of interpretation in supervision*, the interpretive dimension of supervision cannot be replaced, with equivalent effect, by referral to either a training analysis or to any other therapeutic or instructional modality.

This presentation uses a clinical example from my own practice as a supervisor to illustrate the impact and irreplaceable value of such a direct interpretation in supervision. This interpretation was especially striking for a number of reasons. Most important, it demonstrates that interpretation of a resistance in the supervisee can fundamentally alter the therapeutic relationship, enrich the supervisory process, and have unanticipated diagnostic significance. It also revealed an unconscious conflict shared by the patient, by the supervisee, and, unexpectedly, by me. This led to a deeper understanding of my own unacknowledged conflicts and defenses surrounding the issue of interpreting transference in supervision. This example also demonstrates that, when applied with the same appropriateness and tact taken for granted in psychotherapy, concerns that supervisory interpretation will be traumatizing or counterproductive are unwarranted.

CLINICAL EXAMPLE

The Therapist-Supervisee

Dr. A. was a bright, successful fourth-year psychiatric resident in his late twenties, assigned to me for supervision of psychoanalytic psychotherapy for a period of one year. Although he had never been in psychotherapy, he showed a strong ability to think psychologically, had good intuition, and seemed able to communicate well with patients. His personal presentation was unremarkable except for a flamboyant style of dress, mentioned here for reasons to be made clear shortly. I informed Dr. A. of my usual supervisory practice of examining and interpreting both his countertransference with the patient and the transference and countertransference in the supervision to the degree that they relate to the therapy, the supervisory experience, and his growth as an analytic therapist. After some discussion, he agreed to this becoming part of our supervisory contract.

The Patient

Ms. B. was a single woman in her early thirties. Although very bright, she came from a family and cultural environment that emphasized stereotypic, supportive roles for women. In her relationship with her father, she struggled to reveal her competence to him while he insisted that she was weak and required his strength and guidance. This struggle was reflected in her work and personal relationships. In spite of an intelligence that had earned her two university degrees, she was a consistent underachiever and was employed as a secretary. She had developed a contempt for what she viewed as psychological weakness and gravitated to romantic relationships with men she viewed as strong. It should come as no surprise that, invariably, the men were of lesser ability and education than she was, seemed to care little for her, and treated her badly. Although explicitly devalued by her partners, she secretly devalued them as inferior in ability and accomplishment. Her stated aim when she entered therapy was to get help for both her relationship and career difficulties. As chance would have it, Ms. B. was, like Dr. A., a flamboyant dresser.

Supervision and Therapy

When the therapy began, Dr. A. was clearly eager to make good use of the supervision and brought extraordinarily extensive notes to our sessions. It soon became apparent that he expected himself to have an immediate and comprehensive understanding of the patient as a "case," an expectation that was often reflected in facile and premature interpretations. I suspected that this attempt to reassure us of his competence reflected his underlying uncertainty but I did not interpret this directly. Instead, on several occasions, I suggested that his interpretive zeal might reflect his wish to excel and that both supervision and therapy might be better served if he waited to interpret until issues had developed more fully. His enthusiastic acceptance of my suggestion, however, led to no substantive change in his approach to the patient.

As the therapy progressed, Dr. A. and Ms. B. fleshed out a style of relating that indicated a progressing transferential/countertransferential entanglement. They, in their sessions, and he, in our supervision, joked about her outrageous behavior and clothing in a way that betrayed his vicarious participation in her flamboyance. Between themselves, they indulged in mocking exasperation with her counterproductive romantic, social, and professional behavior and shared her unspoken superiority to her peers. Increasingly, they relished sparring with each other. She teasingly admonished him for his stereotypic therapeutic interventions and he teased her about her provocativeness in, and outside, the therapy. Dr. A. and Ms. B. were clearly having a good time but it was unclear to what degree therapy was going on. Ms. B. was repeating her conflicts in the transference, but Dr. A.'s, albeit unconscious, participation in their shared enactment made her repetition unavailable to therapeutic intervention. Their transference/countertransference collusion seemed calculated to obscure, and protect against, a mutual concern about competence and exposure.

While this was happening, grounds for diagnostic and treatment concerns began to emerge. Ms. B.'s rapidly changing, provocative parade of costumes began to border on the bizarre. Within the first several months of therapy, she legally changed her name twice, each name more idiosyncratic and exhibitionistic than the last. She reported a lifelong and serious fantasy that she shared with a childhood girlfriend: as children, they believed they had been the same person in a previous life. As they grew older, this fantasy evolved into their being twins, then siblings, and now friends. Were these and other signs merely the transferential products of an unconventional, imaginative mind, or were they indications of more serious psychological instability? If the latter were true, was she too great a therapeutic challenge for a therapist of Dr. A.'s limited experience? Dr. A. and I discussed these questions in supervision and he showed a genuine concern for Ms. B.'s welfare. However, these discussions and his concern seemed to have little impact on his therapeutic approach. Not only did their continuing enactment forestall clarification of these issues but, more alarming, opportunities multiplied for inadvertent mistakes that might adversely affect the therapy, lead to a therapeutic impasse (Nigram et al. 1977), or even end the therapy altogether.

As one might anticipate, their therapeutic enactment made possible a parallel enactment in our supervision. I felt drawn to share his derision of her transparently self-defeating behavior and also to chide him for his excessive familiarity. We could have easily fallen into our own collusion in which we identified one another as sophisticated therapists who made Ms. B. and her exciting impact on us the pathetic objects of analytic amusement. Instead, I tried to bring the inappropriateness of their interactive style to his attention and to refocus on possible transference meanings. Again, this was well accepted on an academic level but his behavior persisted. With accelerating rapidity, both the therapy and supervision were beginning to feel out of control.

Situations like these often spawn what, in dramatic terms, would be called an inciting incident that, constructively or not, propels the therapy forward. In our case, such an incident was not long in the making. During one of their sessions, Dr. A. interpreted to Ms. B. that she set up self-sabotaging relationships and, to his surprise, she agreed. She said she was only trying to protect herself from a painful sense of secret weakness that a more genuine relationship with a man would reveal. Dr. A. was surprised to find himself overcome by a rush of intense and painful emotion. His face reddened and tears came to his eyes. He quickly recovered his composure and, convinced that she had not seen what had happened, he interpreted, "This isn't you talking. It's your father who feels you're weak and is trying to make you strong."

Dr. A. reported this incident in our next supervisory session. By then, he had devised a defensive explanation for his emotional reaction. With a nod and a wink to Melanie Klein, he described his reaction as an example of a borderline patient "putting feelings into you" via projective identification. I felt intuitively discontent with this glib dismissal of his evidently meaningful emotional experience. I also realized that I had finally had enough of his self-satisfied defensiveness and of my failure to alter his defensive armor with a "learning-difficulty" approach. It was time to interpret their enactment, a sad game which I had allowed to go on too long. I suggested that his explanation, although reflecting a well-known theoretical approach, may be serving to avoid a more personal origin for his feelings by blaming them on Ms. B. I added that, in my opinion, his emotional reaction reflected a transference and countertransference expression of some issue of unconscious concern to both him and Ms. B. I then asked him whether his interpretation to Ms. B. about fathers might also be true of him.

Responsibility dictates that when we make an interpretation we prepare for a reaction, but I was still taken aback by its intensity. Without his moving a muscle or uttering a sound, his face flushed and his eyes filled with tears. He sat motionless, evidently struggling and speechless. After a silence, he regained his composure and said, gravely, that there was a connection he had not been aware of until that moment. I want to emphasize that all this happened without his acknowledging that I may have witnessed anything out of the ordinary. He declined to volunteer additional information and I did not ask for it. But it was clear without his telling me that he had had a profound and sobering insight about himself and that his interpretation did apply to him as well as to Ms. B.

Evidently, Dr. A.'s reaction in the supervision was a repetition of what had occurred with Ms. B. It suddenly struck me that Dr. A. had presented me with an unexpected and pressing dilemma: Should I tell him I had seen his reaction and that it told me he had had an important personal insight? My dilemma came from knowing that Dr. A. had also given no indication that Ms. B. had seen his reaction. In fact, he believed that she had not. But if she had seen it and recognized its importance but said nothing, my silence would parallel an aspect of their collusion. If she had not seen it, disclosing my observation risked interjecting a personal issue of Dr. A.'s into the supervision that would move us inappropriately into an area beyond their therapeutic interaction.

There was no way to avoid this dilemma. Whatever I did or did not do would be an action and would have its effect. For reasons that may reflect my style, both as a therapist and supervisor, and not without misgivings, I chose what felt like valor over discretion. I told him that I had seen his reaction and suspected that he had had an important personal insight. I ventured that avoiding this insight had led to an unacknowledged enactment in which he and Ms. B. identified with each other and which was responsible for an impasse in their therapy and our supervision. Attention to this insight might make their enactment more apparent to him and allow him to more clearly apprehend Ms. B.'s transference. In particular, it might remove his complicity in her treating him as a powerful father surrogate/sparring partner while simultaneously devaluing him as weak and dismissible.

I held my breath. To my relief, my comments seemed to resonate to a depth more profound than previous attempts to alter his behavior. This also brought some relief from my nagging guilt at making the interpretation in the first place, a guilt I felt should not have been there and the existence of which puzzled me. He surprised me further by reflecting, almost immediately, that one aspect of the identification that he could already see was their common flamboyant style. By the end of our supervisory session, it seemed clear that Dr. A. had experienced a fundamental shift in attitude—to Ms. B., to himself, and in his view of his role as her therapist. But my interpretation was to have further, unexpected ramifications both for the therapy and the supervision.

Dr. A. was excited when he arrived at our next supervision. Ms. B., it seemed, had undergone some kind of change. Her usual flippancy had been replaced by an attitude more serious and sober.

As we spoke, I noted that Dr. A. also seemed more serious and listened to me with deeper attention. He related to our supervision and their therapy less as a game or educational stepping stone. I was certain this change resulted from the insight of our previous supervision. Could the change in Ms. B. be connected to the change in him? Could it mean she had seen, and been affected by, his emotion of their previous session? While I was mulling this over, Dr. A. reported that Ms. B., with uncharacteristic sadness, had told him a story about her younger brother, now a man about the same age as Dr. A., who masked vulnerability and unhappiness by feigning a toughness she felt painfully helpless to alter.

It is difficult to capture my reaction to this story in words. I could say that I was speechless—that I was stunned by an insight I could scarcely believe. I could tell you I felt a lump in my throat and tears in my eyes. That a simultaneous wave of relief and poignant sense of exoneration passed over me. That I was embarrassed by this emotional display and watched myself try furiously to hide it from Dr. A. In fact, I registered all these emotions and was simultaneously struck by how similar my entire experience was to what I had witnessed in him just one session before. This parallel would soon explain my relief and exoneration and provided a startling link between me, Dr. A., and Ms. B.

As I began to think more clearly about what had just occurred, I realized that my interpretation to Dr. A., consciously intended only to address their therapeutic impasse, had unconsciously been more profound and comprehensive. Serendipitously, it had given Dr. A. the tools to evaluate Ms. B.'s story in a way that would make clear to him what had just been made clear to me: that she, Dr. A., and I had been unwitting participants in an unconscious drama, one aimed at unraveling our therapeutic impasse and solving our diagnostic dilemma.

As I continued to review the sequence of events in my mind, pivotal elements of the drama fell into place. Because of my interpretation to him, Dr. A. knew in his bones, so to speak, that there was a vulnerability in him for Ms. B. to see because he had already,

independently, recognized and accepted it in himself. This acceptance made it less necessary for him to defensively collude with her
and made him more willing and able to view himself, and to be
viewed by her, as separate. He could now more independently
evaluate whether what she saw in him was distinct from a projection of what she saw in her brother. In other words, he experienced
himself as a more credible witness in general, and about Ms. B. in
particular. Paralleling this in the supervision, my awareness of the
changes in Dr. A. meant that I knew he now had less need to collude
with me. He was now also a more credible witness to me. In other
words, the entire frame through which the two of us looked at each
other and at Ms. B. had altered, and we both knew it. These contentions should surprise no one. They describe what effective interpretations do. That is why we make them.

It was this change in frame that offered us a way through our
therapeutic impasse, allowed me to solve our diagnostic question,
and proved critical to conveying the solution to Dr. A. Without
it, Dr. A. would have remained immersed in his collusion with
Ms. B. and mired in his intellectual defenses. Even if Ms. B. had
told her story, he would be, at best, in the same situation as before—
uncertain whether she could distinguish him from her projections. At worst, Dr. A. would have been swayed, on the theoretical
grounds previously described, to be even more convinced that
she was incapable of such distinctions. I would be no less confused
since, as a vehicle for mediating my understanding of Ms. B., he
would remain too defensive to convincingly inform my intuitions
about her. Neither of us would have had trustworthy information
from which to feel certain of a diagnosis. Our diagnostic dilemma
would continue intact.

Now, however, if Dr. A. actually came to believe that Ms. B.
did distinguish between him and her projections, we both had a
much more solid basis for trusting his belief. This is exactly what
happened—and almost immediately. In the course of that very supervisory session, he realized that he recognized, in her sad mat-
ter-of-factness, the same disengagement from their transferential

enactment that he had already recognized in himself. He understood and could accept that she must have seen his tearfulness and that he had changed by their following session. We both felt convinced that she really was talking about him and that she knew it. Finally, I could convincingly point out to him that his new understanding of Ms. B. solved our diagnostic dilemma: Ms. B. could engage intimately with others with a maturity, sensitivity, and tact beyond that characterized by projective processes.

Why did I experience this process as an unconscious drama? Because it seemed apparent that, similar to the Fates in Greek drama, our unconscious intentions gave us each a part to play through which they would impel us, unwitting, toward their intended goal. That goal was to disrupt the collusion and to find, as if by chance, exactly the information needed to solve our diagnostic dilemma. In this drama, Ms. B. made the first unconscious overture. She admitted, with unusual directness, her reluctance to genuinely engage with men in order to avoid revealing what she viewed as her hidden weaknesses. In response, Dr. A. allowed her overture to penetrate his defense and trigger a visible, if perplexing, emotional response. By rationalizing it with a plausible Kleinian interpretation, he extended the dramatic action to me. Would I side with the collusion by accepting his interpretation or risk exposing it? Unconsciously, he already knew the form my risk would take—I had been careful to tell him that I interpret countertransference. Seeing that I would not avoid interpreting heartened him to face his insight. He let himself know—and he changed. At the same time, by making both his emotional response and subsequent change visible to Ms. B., he extended the dramatic action to her. Would she let herself see it and allow it to inform her understanding and behavior in the therapy? My uncorroborated sense is that Ms. B. saw both his emotion and subsequent change and knew that he no longer needed her to protect him through their collusion. She conveyed that she knew by telling her story about her brother, telling us at the same time that she was available for a different kind of therapeutic relationship. Saying that my interpretation had serendipitously given us this new perspective was simply my conscious experience of that drama's unconscious agenda from the beginning.

Our unconscious drama had allowed both Dr. A. and me to understand that the psychologically fragile persona she brought to therapy was more mask than substance, meant to transferentially convince us that she was as psychologically weak as she and her father would have us believe. She now became less a therapy case to Dr. A., and more a person who, in spite of her own emotional struggles, was aware of him and concerned for him. This different understanding led Dr. A. to a greater sense of optimism that she was capable of truly benefiting from therapy.

Finally, what was the meaning of my relief and sense of exoneration? It meant that, in the face of general peer skepticism and, often, outright disapproval, I had been more vulnerable than I had realized to the usual criticisms of the use of interpretation in supervision. This helped me understand why I generally held off making interpretations until I felt virtually forced into it. My reaction made me more deeply aware that I had been dealing with my own source of insecurity. Insecurity was a supervisory issue for me, as well as a therapeutic issue for them, and my interpretation was a part of my own ongoing process of working through. One could guess that part of the unconscious motivation propelling my interpretation was that Dr. A.'s interpretation about fathers and insecurity evoked a relevant issue for me. One would be right. In the supervision, I only discussed those aspects which pertained to Dr. A. and Ms. B. In retrospect, I regret that I was not more forthcoming, to an appropriate degree, about my own insecurity. It would have further solidified the supervisory alliance had I shared with him that I, too, had vulnerabilities in spite of our different levels of analytic maturity and experience. It would have also given Dr. A. the opportunity to see that vulnerabilities are not necessarily an impediment to following one's therapeutic convictions nor are they incompatible with those convictions bearing fruit.

By the next supervisory session, I noticed that Dr. A.'s clothing choices, though still stylish, had become abruptly less flamboyant. His manner in the supervision had also undergone what would turn out to be a permanent change. He was humbler and more thoughtfully confident. His insight seemed to have increased his appreciation of the profound nature of the psychoanalytic experience and he seemed to have a greater respect for the task that lay before him and Ms. B. At our six-month evaluation, the interpretive work of the previous term was discussed. Dr. A. emphasized how singularly important my interpretation of his countertransference had been to his supervisory experience. He denied that he had experienced it as a boundary violation or that anything inappropriate or intrusive had occurred. He expressed his regret that interpretive work in supervision is not more common.

During the second six months of the supervision, Dr. A.'s work with Ms. B. showed an increased depth of understanding made possible by our interpretive work. He was better able to see his general need to identify narcissistically with his patients and he continued to struggle with this need in his therapy with her. His greater comfort with their separateness and differences made him more aware of how critical and uncomprehending he was of Ms. B.'s unwillingness to make maximal use of her abilities. This awareness of his lack of comprehension led him to attempt to understand life from her point of view. It also brought into focus his own need for acclaim, a need which, we both acknowledged, could not be more fully investigated in supervision but could be further elucidated in a personal therapy.

DISCUSSION

In exploring the merits of supervisory interpretation, one must not get bogged down in whether or not learning analytic psychotherapy extends beyond countertransference issues. In either case, countertransference certainly plays a pivotal, obstructive role and its exposure increases the supervisee's knowledge and psychological growth. What is being argued here is not that interpreting countertransference should be obligatory or relentlessly pursued. It is that to censure it by fiat is unwarranted and robs patient, supervisee, and supervisor of an irreplaceable, potential benefit. As in analytic psychotherapy, the use of interpretation in its supervision is invaluable when guided by appropriateness, tact, and relevance.

The usual reasons for excluding interpretation from the supervisory process can be summarized by the contention that interpretation blurs the boundary assumed to exist between supervision and psychotherapy and confuses their essentially distinct, incompatible clinical purposes and methods (Ekstein and Wallerstein 1972). More specifically, it is claimed that interpretation evokes therapeutic regression—necessary for psychotherapy but incompatible with effective supervisory instruction. Interpretation is said to assume a nonjudgmental approach, necessary for psychotherapy but incompatible with supervisory teaching and evaluative obligations. Without the safeguards implicit in the psychotherapeutic frame, it is claimed that interpretation may become "wild" or inappropriate, intruding upon and eventually undermining a potentially constructive teaching process. Taken together, it is maintained that these factors not only undermine the supervisory process but subvert the evolution of a collegial relationship between supervisor and supervisee, an important part of the supervisee's maturing professional identification.

Yet, when the interpretive work in the case vignette is examined, it is difficult to sustain these contentions. Carefully restricting interpretation to its proper and relevant focus, applying the usual evidential requirements (Lester and Robertson 1995), and employing the tact and sensitivity that accompany all responsible interpretation seemed to avoid these pitfalls. There is no evidence that Dr. A. experienced the interpretive work as anything but beneficial to the supervision, that an inappropriate intrusion occurred, or that a supposed boundary was blurred (Gorman 1996).

Quite the contrary, his responses indicate that he viewed the interpretive work as enhancing the supervision and well within the supervisory task. From a more general supervisory point of view, it also allowed Dr. A. to deepen and consolidate his understanding of the countertransferential process and how it can express itself in collusive behavior.

At the six-month evaluation, Dr. A. treated the interpretive thread as a normal part of the supervision and he discussed its role in his development as a therapist in a perfectly straightforward manner. He exhibited no signs of conflict between the interpretive and the evaluative dimension of supervision because the restricted use of interpretation was viewed as a tool in the service of his growth as a therapist. The nonjudgmental spirit of interpretation complemented, rather than undermined, the evaluative component of supervision. Of course, much of this depended on Dr. A.'s confidence that the interpretive work would not extend to an open-ended exploration of his personal life. The creation of this confidence relied heavily on how the interpretive issue was handled from the outset. Interpretation was openly discussed as part of the supervisory contract and his permission for its use was obtained. Confidence was further reinforced by the supervisor consistently honoring the intent of the interpretive contract, and by avoiding interpretation in areas of no clear relevance to the supervised therapy or by pursuing interpretation into relevant areas of clear discomfort to Dr. A.

Strictly adhering to the interpretive focus of the supervision and interpreting only when evidence seems compelling precludes wild interpretation from being any more likely in supervision than in psychotherapy. As long as supervision and psychotherapy share the same care to avoid "inferential leaps" (Lester and Robertson 1995, p. 218), the risk of inappropriate or wild interpretations is of no great concern. Restricting interpretation to issues of clear relevance to the supervision also minimizes regression, so that Dr. A. could safely focus on the learning task at hand.

Too exclusive a focus on the risks of interpretation may unwittingly convey disrespect for the supervisee's professional and personal maturity. Treating supervisees as competent and expected to benefit from the appropriate examination of their unconscious processes is a mark of collegial respect and encourages legitimate pride and gratitude. A supervisory approach that treats the supervisee as too fragile to tolerate interpretation can be experienced as condescending, patronizing, and demeaning, ironically undermining collegiality rather than reinforcing it. I would argue that this case illustrates that collegiality was not only maintained but enhanced by integrating relevant interpretation into the supervisory process. It is further enhanced if the supervisor is willing to symmetrically reveal his or her own countertransference in the supervision. So long as interpretation is applied to both supervisee and supervisor as an investigative tool in the service of the supervision, collegiality becomes associated with a more profound humility. Understanding, born of the *experience* that patient, supervisee, and supervisor are all vulnerable to unconscious influence, enhances effective clinical work.

This common vulnerability, conveyed most deeply by the use of interpretation, is the most helpful way to conceptualize and convey the parallel process. Putting the parallel process in the context of transference and countertransference makes it understandable as a natural, if initially surprising, consequence of more fundamental psychodynamic processes and allows it to be seamlessly incorporated into broader psychoanalytic theory. Attempting to conceptualize and treat countertransferences as learning problems contributes to the less theoretically satisfying view of parallel process as a new, initially disturbing, and inscrutable psychoanalytic entity particular to supervision.

Is it possible that, in other hands, the usual noninterpretive methods would have made interpretation unnecessary? In my opinion, the interpretation altered Dr. A.'s understanding of himself and his dynamic in the therapeutic and supervisory relationships more profoundly than didactic interventions did or could have. This is to assert no more than what, in the context of psychotherapy, would be considered self-evident. Neither was the change in him merely a shrewd behavioral modification for my benefit. His altered understanding and relation toward Ms. B was maintained for the remainder of the supervision, and changes to his general manner and style have continued to the present time.

The interpretation made to Dr. A. was mild in its depth and was anything but relentlessly pursued. Some might argue that it was hardly an interpretation at all. However, it satisfies the criteria for an interpretation, in that it made sense of a symptomatic response and brought insight to Dr. A.'s unconscious countertransference. There is an implicit tendency among psychoanalytic psychotherapists to take the phrase "interpretation of transference" to refer to the kind of deep, general, and reconstructive interpretation that forms a very small, albeit crucial, part even of a psychoanalysis (Lester and Robertson 1995). This extreme view of what qualifies as interpretation is being increasingly challenged (Lester and Robertson 1995, Renik 1993). In any case, such an interpretation would have been inappropriate to a supervisory mandate and Dr. A. would probably have felt it to be so. For residents like Dr. A., appropriate supervisory interpretations may be the only time they subjectively experience, to however limited a degree, the power of the interpretations that they are certain to make in their practices, and their only clinical training in the importance of analyzing countertransference. For certain residents, it may even tip the balance toward pursuing their own analytic therapy.

In the above case, the potential helpfulness of deeper and more thorough interpretation was addressed by suggesting a personal therapy. However, the fuller exploration that such a therapy might provide is not a substitute for interpretation in the supervision (Gorman 1996). A personal therapy, isolated from the supervision, would be unlikely to evoke Dr. A.'s emotions with precisely the same quality as did the supervised therapy. Exploration in a personal therapy could not have captured the immediate relevance to his work with Ms. B. because the personal therapy does not have the same agenda or mandate.

CONCLUSION

That clinical, psychoanalytic data can so easily be adapted to support any number of theoretical perspectives makes it unreasonable to expect that the arguments presented here will convince everyone. I would view this presentation as successful if it encourages supervisors to attempt to verify its conclusions in their own supervisions. I believe that attempts in this direction will go a long way toward confirming the merits of interpreting transference and countertransference in the supervision of psychoanalytic psychotherapy.

REFERENCES

Eitingon, M. (1926). An address to the international training commission. *International Journal of Psycho-Analysis* 7:130–134.

Ekstein, R., and Wallerstein, R. S. (1972). *The Teaching and Learning of Psychotherapy*. Madison, CT: International Universities Press.

Goin, M. K., and Kline, F. (1976). Countertransference: a neglected subject in clinical supervision. *American Journal of Psychiatry* 133:41–44.

Gorman, H. E. (1996). Interpretation of transference in psychoanalytic psychotherapy. *Free Associations* 39:379–402.

Kovacs, V. (1936). Training and control-analysis. *International Journal of Psycho-Analysis* 17:346–354.

Lester, E. P., and Robertson, B. M. (1995). Multiple interactive processes in psychoanalytic supervision. *Psychoanalytic Inquiry* 15:211–225.

Nigram, T., Cameron, P. M., and Leverette, J. S. (1977). Impasses in the supervisory process: a resident's perspective. *American Journal of Psychotherapy* 51(2):252–272.

Renik, O. (1993). Analytic interaction: conceptualizing technique in the light of the analyst's irreducible subjectivity. *Psychoanalytic Quarterly* 62:553–572.

Schlesinger, H. J. (1995). Supervision for fun and profit: or how to tell if the fun is profitable. *Psychoanalytic Inquiry* 15:190–210.

Searles, H. (1955). The informational value of the supervisor's emotional experiences. *Psychiatry* 18:135–146.

When Supervisor and Therapist Dream

The Use of an Unusual Countertransference Phenomenon*

ANNE E. BERNSTEIN AND SUSAN C. KATZ

The supervisory situation is a very complex triadic relationship among supervisor, supervisee, and patient. It allows for multiple countertransference paradigms to exist in dynamic fluctuation: supervisee and patient, supervisee and supervisor, and supervisor and patient.

Freud (1900) was willing to share his dream about a patient in order to teach about dream interpretation. The specimen or Irma dream, the first dream of its kind to be subjected to intense scrutiny, is a countertransference dream (Erickson 1954). Through the analysis of this dream, Freud revealed some of his own conflicts and modes of defense. Of the fifty dreams reported by Freud, patients appear in the manifest content of three. Analysts probably use their dreams privately to understand their patients, and ana-

*The authors wish to express their gratitude to Baba Moody, MSW, and the social worker staff at the Psychiatric Institute to whom this paper was initially presented and for whose thoughtful discussion we are grateful.

lytic candidates would be expected to report dreams related to their work to their training analysts. Yet, aside from Freud, very few analysts have been willing to report their dreams about patients (Gitelson 1952, Kleeman 1962, Lester 1985, Orr 1954, Tauber 1954, Tower 1956, Whitman et al. 1963).

In 1969 Whitman and colleagues documented in their sleep laboratory studies that dreams about the patient were occurring more frequently in analysts and therapists than was being reported. They studied countertransference in dreams and experimentally recovered dreams of psychiatric residents in treatment and dreams of therapists not in treatment or supervision.

They noted that all of the reported dreams represent countertransference in the broadest sense. They stressed that these dreams were invariably helpful in producing insight and illuminating the treatment process. Emch (1955) makes the point in reference to analytic candidates that the supervisor must believe that the supervisee would be able to deal with countertransference issues as well as the supervisor if her own countertransferences were called into question. We believe that it is necessary for the supervisor, even in the supervision of psychoanalytic psychotherapy, to trust her supervisees in this regard and to convey this message openly if we are not to lose valuable countertransference data.

Little (1957), in discussing the analyst's total reaction to the patient, notes that the analyst has to bear tension and discharge but also know that there are some things the analyst cannot stand. Countertransference manifestations when discussed openly allow for the differentiation between anxiety and panic, between the analyst's own anxiety and the fear of the patient's anxiety. We would extend this formulation to psychoanalytic psychotherapy and further to the supervisors of both psychoanalysis proper and psychoanalytic psychotherapy.

Langs (1984) writes that dreams may be reported by the supervisee if there is a highly disturbing problem with the supervisor, problems in the supervisee's life, or unusual problems with a patient. Kanzer (1955) repeats Freud's suggestion that the dream is told to the person for whom it is meant. This would seem to imply that if a dream is told to the supervisor, Lang's first hypothesis about a disturbed supervisory relationship might be correct. Sachel (1982) implies that in the supervisory process one must be aware that the countertransferences are complex.

We have found no literature that discusses the psychodynamics that might be involved when the supervisor dreams about the patient. It is either a coincidence or hitherto unreported circumstance when both supervisor and supervisee dream about the patient, or, as in the case to be reported, dream about the patient's dreams. Ekstein and Wallerstein (1958) have a view very similar to our own. They describe the parallel process going on in both supervisor and supervisee and stress the need for the dyad to look at the problems of both the learner and the teacher.

In the spirit of the last formulations, we wish to present the patient's history and selections from verbatim process material drawn from two supervisory sessions. They include some of the patient's dreams. In addition we will present the dreams of both the supervisor and supervisee that were shared. The understanding of these helped clarify the dynamics of the patient, the transference, and the countertransference, and furthered the therapeutic work.

The dreams of both were most probably related to the patient's outpouring of unconscious material and to the anxiety evoked in the supervisee confronted by this, as well as the anxiety in the supervisor who wished to help the supervisee to become more comfortable.

We suspect that what was required for this evidently rare type of sharing in the supervisory process was a fine tuning of the therapist's and patient's unconscious, as well as the unconscious of the supervisor. The tuning of the unconscious of the supervisor and patient was achieved via the verbatim session material from therapist to supervisor. In addition, the supervisor and supervisee had to have established a supervisory alliance not unlike the therapeutic alliance that must be forged between patient and therapist. Benedek and Fleming (1983) have written extensively about the powerful interactions involved in psychoanalytic supervision. We believe that these are similar to the interactions involved in the supervision of psychoanalytic psychotherapy.

CASE STUDY

Lynn was seen in psychoanalytically oriented psychotherapy twice a week. She is a 33-year-old administrator, divorced for several years. Her religious background is Fundamentalist. She lives with her fiancé, Timothy, had been in treatment for panic attacks for one year, and was routinely referred to one of the authors as a clinic patient. The problems she presented involved conflicts about marriage. On the one hand, she was terrified of getting married and on the other hand, the goal she had was to get married and have a baby as soon as possible, if not immediately. Another problem she disclosed was trouble with separation. She has had a boyfriend, Terry, for some years who was verbally abusive and made her feel unworthy and "like a bad person." Lynn had tried to separate from him repeatedly for three years, and when she finally moved out, started having panic attacks. She was still trying to officially break up with him.

Lynn is the second of six children, five girls and one boy. Significant in her development is that by the age of 3 months she had been weaned from breast to bottle and to skim milk from a cup because of obesity. She remembered her mother as being continually pregnant, overworked, and depressed. Her father was extremely active in the church, which took up his evenings. She was a spirited toddler and remembered having terrible temper tantrums if she didn't get her own way or enough attention. This changed when she was about six years old on the occasion of her hospitalization for rheumatic fever. She believed that she might die as a punishment for her temper. Earlier she was converted to a Fundamentalist church because she knew she'd burn in Hell if she didn't. She remembered knowing that she had to seek forgiveness because of her terrible temper.

Lynn was a good child during latency. She remembered that her parents liked to show off all the little girls dressed perfectly in church. She had a troubled adolescence, however. Her family sought family therapy for a few months after a sister became pregnant out of wedlock and was put out of the house. Lynn then started to act up a lot. She almost got married at 18 and decided not to, realizing she was too young. At age 24 she married a childhood sweetheart, John, but they "discovered" that he was gay when they came to New York and divorced about a year later.

A year after her divorce she developed major depression and was in therapy twice a week working on her dissatisfaction with her career decisions, general difficulty making decisions, and problems in relationships with men. She fled that treatment after three years. Soon afterwards she met Terry with whom she had so much difficulty breaking up.

The section from the verbatim supervisory session that follows had the following background. The patient had quit smoking after her last session without discussing her plan to do so. It was a sign to her that she was able to be in control and grown up. With the loss of that gratification she experienced a great deal of anxiety. She had made her final break with Terry and was living with Timothy in a less chaotic, more ego-supportive relationship and was presenting a lot of dreams.

Supervisory Session One

The patient started by saying: "I'm finding it more difficult not smoking. It doesn't get easier. I've had a lot of dreams. You were in one of them. I was looking for an apartment with Timothy. Another couple was with us. There were four bedrooms. The couple had a kid with a talking Cabbage Patch doll. I was grossed out by the doll but I spoke to it. John [her former husband] was there. He pulled me into a closet. He and I were going to jump out and scare people. I also dreamed there was going to be a nuclear war. People knew because there were lots of planes, all flying towards Washington. There was skywriting: it said, 'Go into a place without windows. Find a solid chair and sit in it.' I remembered thinking that that would prevent me from dying. Finally, I got a great apartment and we had a nuclear war.

"Tuesday night, you [the therapist] were really in my dreams. I was mowing my parent's backyard and covering it with carpeting. There was a big building. I was going to meet you on the roof for therapy but we couldn't have the room to ourselves, there was someone else in there. Then it got weird. We went to an amphitheatre to see a 59 to 60-year-old cowboy rock singer, country western singer. He was running up to the front. I was walking up to the front to get to the door and run out. There was an overhang with something on it that I was looking at. It was a bomb. It was metal and wired like a bomb. Then you were there. My engagement ring started to fall apart and you had to help me put the ring back together. I saw it was loose and tried to pull it apart to keep the stone safe. It came apart like splinters, and then fell apart like a five-part fishhook. We couldn't get it back together. I was afraid of looking for the diamond.

"Last night, I dreamed that a cat had all these kittens, seven of them. The house was set away from where I lived. Someone asked, 'Where are you going to keep them?' It was a nurse. I saw the mother cat. I went to see the kittens. They were 6 weeks old. They were unusual looking. One was pretty and gray with curly fur. Two were mostly black and white. One was very unusual with gray curly fur. He was dragging his right side. The three most unusual kittens were in a basket. They were dead, dried up. They were brown like a snake's shed skin with a spine inside. I thought, 'How strange. I guess they were too unusual to live.' Then a healthy cat appeared. It was black and it came and sat by me and I was petting it. Three died, four were alive. Three out of seven lived. Seven is the number of times my mother had been pregnant. One time she had a miscarriage. One cat died."

Therapist: Three of your mother's living children had shells? [like the snake-shed skin]

Patient: Me and my sister may have been my mother's kids. We were louder, more rebellious. Margo got lost in the shuffle. She wished my mother liked her more. We all felt a compulsion to do the opposite of what she said. The other three kids were moderately religious. They were balanced. They integrated their personalities better. Maybe they are the ones who have the shells.

Therapist: What would have been dried up in them?

Patient: I don't know.

Therapist: Let's look back to the dream. What was left was a condom? [The therapist interprets the shell as a condom.]

Patient: Would what was lost be a penis? There's also three without children now. The unusual ones all died. Julie, Liz, and Douglas were middle-of-the-road. Two who died actually had paw prints on them. (The patient laughed.)

Therapist: What are you laughing at?

Patient: The mother got her hands on me. The cats had white hand marks in their fur. The gray one with curly hair who had a stroke would be Lisa. She was drab and gray and she was afraid to speak in public, afraid of cats.

Therapist: What about the mother cat?

Patient: It was missing.

Therapist: Is this dream about me? I seem to be a cat in your dreams. (Reference to past dream in which Katz became cats.)

Patient: Maybe if it had been about you, I would have had the first dream. John and I were acting like kids because we were jumping out of closets to scare people because we really were kids. Timothy and I were there as we are now. There was a fourth person . . . the couple with the Cabbage Patch kid. It was me when I was older. I wasn't happy about living with them. I didn't want to share. I don't want to get older. I don't like the whole thing. It means dying. I don't care about wrinkles but the end result is frightening. In the dream with the little girl and her doll, they were my kids. I wish I could stay this age a long time and put off having kids. I was reading a book about the lack of feeling fully adult. I ate lunch with Joan who is having it out with her husband. I asked her what would happen if they had kids too soon? I'm afraid of being adult and more responsible, having to be consistently giving; I like sleeping late and all night. Timothy is an adult; maybe I'm hoping he'll do it all.

Therapist: Is that realistic?

Patient: If I'm not capable of being a parent, there's always Timothy.

Therapist: Maybe he senses that and he's scared.

Patient: He has said I'm spoiled and I like things my way. I don't like extra work. He knows I don't do 50 percent now. I don't know what he's feeling. I work longer. I get home later. It's important to be consistent and always available emotionally. I know physically I can run away.

Therapist: Like in the dream when you ran out of the auditorium and see a bomb which blows up your ring. Do you think I have motives to keep your engagement together?

Patient: I was able to keep it together because I'm seeing you. I left Terry in the first place. I feel this is a better relationship than the others I've had. A large part of me thinks it's really good. That part of me wants to keep him, more than my feelings that I want to blow it apart. Someone who'll make me lunch to take to work.

Therapist: That's a mommy.

Patient: Yeah, he does it better so I'm happy to have him do it. I am confused about being male or female. I could be the mother or the father. Timothy said he won't be a wife. When I was little, I was told I couldn't do things because I was a girl. If I was a boy, I'd have more options. Real early, I was given to understand that we had to be clothed. Little girls couldn't run around without T-shirts but boys could. I knew it was better without the shirt. I knew something was wrong with my body. It would have been a way to be special, distinctive. I remember feeling that I wanted to have to do things. I'm afraid a pattern will come into place and I won't do it well. If you don't do it well, you're bad, embarrassing. When I would cook, Terry responded weirdly, like I'd done something wrong.

Supervisor: We're hearing a lot of dreams that reveal a great deal about her psychodynamics.

Therapist: The chair that she sits in is in the session room—is one that rocks—she has a 'sitting-in-the-rocking-chair' way of being safe from atomic attack and had the rock concert and dream in which her engagement ring blows up: those are important details.

Supervisor: Let's talk about details and what they tell us about where she stands. She is the Cabbage Patch doll that grossed her out.

Therapist: What about the violence in her dreams: nuclear war, rock concert?

Supervisor: The mother cat wasn't there for starters.

Therapist: Her associations with kittens were mixed in but the kittens came in two varieties as her siblings. Abnormal ones and three normal, middle-of-the-road: conformist and nonconformist cats. Nonconformist cats shed their skins: that's about her. Her competition with siblings, her problems with mother being pregnant all the time and unavailable. She has feelings about castration, loss of the condom, penis, and the Cabbage Patch Kid who is not a real kid but some bizarre something else.

Supervisor: The themes and associations have to do with material about deprivation, violence, rage, and castration.

SUPERVISORY SESSION TWO

Therapist: The patient begins the hour by saying: "I stopped smoking, now I'm depressed. I'm short-tempered. I have to hold myself in check. Maybe I'm really angry and incompetent. Maybe this is really me. I got very irritated with my supervisor. I dreamed I was going through Timothy's drawers. He asked what I was doing. I told him none of your business. I don't know why I was doing it. We were living in a tropical country. You could see in. I wanted to see everything he owned. Friday evening I was severely depressed. Timothy was working. Visions of suicide passed through my mind. I could just jump out the window and not have to worry about whether I smoked or not or whether I'm competent at work. I thought of the pros and cons. I was very angry at my mother as a kid and as a teenager. I don't remember feeling this angry here before.'"

Supervisor: She is angry at you for having taken away her cigarettes. She is looking for her cigarettes, penis, literally, in Timothy's drawers.

Therapist: She sees me as the one who took away the bottle and gave her the cup of skim milk. That was a major deprivation for her as a child. When she gave up smoking, she started to feel very different at work.

Therapist: I want to tell you about a very peculiar piece of behavior that she's developed in the session. She started to suck her pinky finger.

Patient: I had a dream of Ohio. Terry was living with his wife next door to my parents. I drove up in a red, 4000-cubic-centimeter car—a Camaro—a hot car with a stick shift. I had a GTO when I was home. I remember talking to him and his wife. Really, dreams of my old boyfriend?

Therapist: What does it mean to drive a red Camaro? Who drives a red Camaro?

Patient: Race car drivers. To have owned it at 19 would have meant I was cool. Owning it then meant to me and others driving fast, tempting fate, not a lot of concern, some sort of power thing. For me it has to do with independence. It's not a car my parents would own. Being able to get away from my parents.

I was afraid I would attack them. I was afraid of my own power with my mother, telling her she's a bad mother, a lot of things you could say to her. Doug said it when he was a baby. I'm afraid to say it to her. There's no gray, just black and white. She's terrible. If a 10-year-old said it to her and she got upset, how would it be if I said it to her now?

Therapist: So the explosion in your dream has to do with what a bad mother your mother was.

Patient: And Father was a total waste and wasn't there either (she was sucking her pinkie at this point). The danger to Timothy is that I make him a mother. I remember thinking that wouldn't do it. That was a false hope. It's not a guarantee. It was . . . it was . . . we really die anyway. I think of running. I'm afraid of getting married; I want to run. I do make him into my mother. I'm trying to precipitate something. I said to him, 'What if I decided to go away for a couple of months?" I have to do something. I'm looking for an excuse to say this isn't going to work, starting a fight around an independent issue.

   (The patient presented two other elaborate dreams in this session with similar themes.)

Supervisor: Let's recapitulate, because the dreams come one on top of the other. This session starts with the first dream which is of going through Timothy's drawers. The second dream is about the red Camaro with the stick shift. Now the question is, What impulses is she trying to contend with and what are her unconscious defensive maneuvers in order to try to repair the damage that she so clearly feels? It occurred to me that I had a dream about this patient. My dream was: I was working in the pediatric emergency room, something I did as a pediatrician. What comes in but a Cabbage Patch Kid with a cast on its leg and something is wrong with this cast and I have to see what it is and figure out how to get the cast on correctly. I understand the day residue to my dream, and my associations mean that this is a patient with penis envy (Karme 1981), the fantasy of an illusory penis (Bernstein and Warner 1984, Parens 1971), and all kinds of other body image problems that came out of both the patient's dreams and mine of the Cabbage Patch Kid."

Therapist: I had a dream after this session also. I was sitting, I think it was in a little red sports car, and a woman was driving. I was in the passenger seat and she drove off a bridge, on purpose, into the water, and as we were falling down I was trying to get out of the car and she was trying to keep me in so that we would both drown.

Supervisor: You were sensing a negative transference and also have a perception that she has the ability to grab on and to hold on. She reached the unconscious of both of us. For you it was the subject of separation from someone who's trying to hold on and be destructive, for me it's her castration anxiety.

DISCUSSION

This patient has regressed from phallic oedipal issues to the theme of destructive rage at her depriving mother. Lynn did not have a good enough mother (Winnicott 1965), a present, available, and optimally frustrating mother. The therapist's dream focused on the regressive reparative fantasies of the patient that evoked serious countertransference anxiety. The supervisor's dream led to an awareness of the patient's acute castration anxiety.

The therapist felt more comfortable in helping the patient to face the phallic symbolic aspects of her losses: cigarette smoking, her boyfriend Terry, as well as the divorce that had led to her first major depression. This is so-called "analysis from the top down." The therapist accepted the supervisor's suggestion to focus on these issues. As a result both the dream and affective flooding were stemmed. By the end of the supervisory period the therapist was helping the patient to analyze the negative maternal transference that by this time was less overwhelming for them both.

CONCLUSION

A firm supervisory alliance can allow for exchange of unconscious material in the spirit of sharing the conscious and unconscious operations of both the learner and the teacher. Judging by the paucity of literature on the subject, it would seem that we are reporting either an uncommon occurrence or an uncommonly shared one. It is our hope that our candor will enable other therapist/ supervisor teams to report similar work. The elements that allow for such a mutually honest interaction require understanding and encouragement, for the work that emerges is most helpful to the patient, therapist, and supervisor.

REFERENCES

Benedek, T., and Fleming, J. (1983). *Psychoanalytic Supervision: A Model of Clinical Training.* New York: International Universities Press.

Bernstein, A., and Warner, G. M. (1981). *An Introduction to Contemporary Psychoanalysis.* New York: Jason Aronson.

———. (1984). *Women Treating Women.* New York: International Universities Press.

Ekstein, R., and Wallerstein, R. (1958). *The Teaching and Learning of Psychotherapy.* New York: International Universities Press.

Emch, M. (1955). Social context of supervision. *International Journal of Psycho-Analysis* 36:298–306.

Erikson, E. H. (1954). The dream specimen of psychoanalysis. *Journal of the American Psychoanalytic Association* 2:5–56.

Freud, S. (1900). The interpretation of dreams. *Standard Edition* 4/5.

Gitelson, H. (1952). The emotional position of the analyst in the psychoanalytic situation. *International Journal of Psycho-Analysis* 33:1–10.

Kanzer, M. (1955). The communicative function of the dream. *International Journal of Psycho-Analysis* 36:260–266.

Karme, L. (1981). Penis envy. *Journal of the American Psychoanalytic Association* 4:563–574.

Kleeman, J. A. (1962). Dreaming for a dream course. *Psychoanalytic Quarterly* 31:203–231.

Langs, R. (1984). Supervisory crises and dreams from supervision.

In *Clinical Perspectives on the Supervision of Psychoanalysis and Psychotherapy*, ed. L. Caligor, P. M. Bromberg, and J. D. Meltzer, pp. 107–141. New York: Plenum.

Lester, E. (1985). The female analyst and the erotized transference. *International Journal of Psycho-Analysis* 66:283–293.

Little, M. (1957). "R"—the analyst's total response to his patient's needs. *International Journal of Psycho-Analysis* 58:240–254.

Orr, D. W. (1954). Transference and countertransference. a historical survey. *Journal of the American Psychoanalytic Association* 2:621–670.

Parens, H. (1971). A contribution of separation-individuation in the development of psychic structure. In *Separation-Individuation: Essays in Honor of Margaret S. Mahler*, ed. J. B. McDevitt and C. F. Settlage, pp. 100–112. New York: New York University Press.

Sachel, M. (1982). Supervision dynamic in psychotherapy. In *Applied Science in Psychotherapy*, ed. M. Blumfield, pp. 5–43. New York: Grune & Stratton.

Tauber, E. S. (1954). Exploring the therapeutic use of countertransference data. *Psychiatry* 17:331–336.

Tower, L. E. (1956). Countertransference. *Journal of the American Psychoanalytic Association* 4:224–255.

Whitman, R. M., Kramer, M., and Baldridge, B. J. (1963). Experimental study of supervisors of psychotherapy. *Archives of General Psychiatry* 9:527–535.

———. (1969). Dreams about patient: approach to problem countertransference. *Journal of the American Psychoanalytic Association* 17:702–727.

Winnicott, D. (1965). The theory of parent–infant relationship. *International Journal of Psycho-Analysis* 4:235–236.

Transference–Countertransference Dynamics and Disclosure in Supervision[1]

WILLIAM J. COBURN

INTRODUCTION

In the tradition of psychoanalysis, the vital supervision experience is second only to treatment itself in developing the knowledge, skills, intuition, and self-organization of the professional clinician. The natural application[2] of psychoanalytic art and science seeks

---

1. Originally published in the *Bulletin of the Menninger Clinic*, Winter, 1997; a modified version of this chapter was delivered at the 40th Annual Winter Meeting of the American Academy of Psychoanalysis in Scottsdale, Arizona, 1996. I wish to thank Dr. James L. Fosshage for his support and helpful comments and want to acknowledge Dr. Philip Ringstrom for his insightful recommendations. I am also deeply grateful to Dr. Estelle Shane for her provision of a new object experience in the supervision setting, and I want to thank Dr. Joanne Moran for her poignant examples of reflection with a toleration for not knowing.
2. By natural, I mean the quality of those relations and interactions with the patient that are not artificial or manufactured, but that emerge from within the therapist as a logical result of his essential being-as-therapist, in contrast to acting-as-therapist.

to ameliorate psychopathology and develop and enhance one's personal freedom, meaning, and authenticity. The potential for realizing this natural application originates, in order of importance, from one's own treatment experience, one's supervision experience, and one's academic experience. I wish to focus on the second of the three domains, as examining more closely those processes inherent in the supervision setting that can further enhance the clinician's effectiveness with patients.

Parallels have often been drawn between the therapeutic relationship and the supervision relationship (Searles 1965), even though tradition has maintained the need for their diversity in character and separateness in application (see Lewin and Ross 1960, regarding "syncretic dilemma"). In some instances, one is antithetical to the other. In others, distinctions between the two evaporate.[3] Examining the similarities and parallels of the two types of relationships can deepen the supervisor–supervisee relationship, as well as expand the supervisor's and supervisee's subjective sense of the patient.

In that vein, the value of the supervision relationship resides not just in the enhancement of the supervisee's clinical effectiveness, but also in its potential for providing a developmental or "new object experience" (Shane and Shane 1989) for the supervisee, vis-à-vis his professional identity, self-experience, and self-organization. Shane and Shane (1989) address this developmental dimension in the context of the analytic relationship, stating that "it is always a case of the messenger being assimilated along with the message" (p. 335). Alternatively stated, "the here-and-now unique analytic

---

3. I am not espousing a merger of the two types of relationships, in contrast to the Hungarian system associated with Kovacs (1936), in which it was recommended that one's analyst also function as one's supervisor. Rather, I wish to highlight their similarities from an experiential and dynamic viewpoint. At a given moment, the ambiance of the supervision relationship could assume the *experience* of psychotherapy when, for example, a supervisee is exploring and illuminating his countertransference configuration in relation to the patient under discussion.

relationship *in itself* has developmental power, stimulating development via the patient's experience of the analyst" (p. 334). This dimension of experience is present, optimally, in the context of the supervision relationship as well.

THE SUPERVISION RELATIONSHIP

The essential dynamics and experiences in the supervision relationship often determine the character and direction of the therapy of the patient under consideration. The supervisor and supervisee continually grope and explore the proverbial elephant, and considerations of who has hold of the more accurately representative part is often controversial and debatable, if not political. The more pluralistic, contemporary supervisor may tend to assume a higher degree of sophistication and vision in his supervisee, as a function of his *experience*, and may convey a greater sense of parity by eliminating notions of final authority and arbiters of the "truth" (i.e., a two-person model). Conversely, the more singular, classical supervisor may tend to feel that the "truth" about the patient is primarily fixed, static, and discoverable (archeological model) and that in light of his respectable and advanced level of training, education, and experience, he (the supervisor) is ultimately the determiner of the shape of the elephant.

I would like to posit three fundamental tenets of the supervision experience: (1) that the primary—though not sole—subject matter of the relationship is the "unfolding, illumination, and transformation" of a third party's [the patient's] subjective world (Stolorow et al. 1987, p. 9) and the way in which the therapist may be instrumental in promoting that process; (2) that the relational phenomena between the supervisor and the supervisee that arise out of continued contact and discussion—including the convictions about the patient that are mutually developed, shared, and maintained—are determined by the natural and complex transference–countertransference configurations and interplay among the three participants; and (3) that the exploration and examination of the nature of these relational phenomena comprise what is potentially most valuable to the supervisee's—and the patient's—development and progress. It is the second and third dimensions especially that I wish to explore.

INTERSUBJECTIVITY THEORY

In examining and conceptualizing the supervision relationship and process, the utilization of an intersubjective framework is particularly conducive to understanding more clearly the vital, transformative characteristics inherent in this setting. This specific application of intersubjectivity theory has not been widely discussed. Fosshage's (1995) revealing paper regarding self psychological and intersubjective perspectives on supervision provides a notable exception. Fosshage clearly delineates the potential "listening perspectives" of the supervisor and highlights the theoretical and clinical utility of listening from "within" the perspective of the subject—that is, the centrality of adopting an "empathic mode of perception" when attempting to illuminate the perspectives of patient and supervisee. This experience-near approach contrasts significantly with the more traditional orientations toward supervision and emphasizes how transference–countertransference configurations and experiences of the three participants are co-determined by all three intersecting subjectivities, not just primarily the patient's transference dynamics.

Another informative exception is found in Ricci's (1995) treatment of the supervision process through the use of an "empathic, affect-attuned, intersubjective model" (p. 60). He addresses the concept of parallel process viewed through the lens of affects, motivation, and intersubjective phenomena. He also underscores the centrality of tracking continually the self-state of the supervisee and of being mindful of his current particular foreground motivational system. The promotion and maintenance of self-cohesiveness in the supervisee, as with the patient, afford the supervisee experiences characterized by exploration and openness in contrast to aversion and withdrawal in which the danger exists of "the [supervision] process, thus vitiated, becom[ing] an 'as if' learning situation" (Ricci 1995, p. 64).

In general, intersubjectivity theory, as addressed by these authors, helps structure the use of an experience-near perspective and a two-person (or, in this case, a three-person) model to understand and enhance the supervision process. Stolorow (1995) states that "the trajectory of self-experience is shaped at every point in development by the intersubjective system in which it crystallizes" (p. 394). Continually focusing on the nature of each participant's contributions to the tripartite system and the corresponding self-experiences of all three participants encourages a deeper illumination of those factors that are responsible for the development of the patient and hopefully of the supervisee as well.

CAPACITY FOR REFLECTION

Research in psychology and psychoanalysis underscores the salience and need for reflectivity in both the supervisor and supervisee (Neufeldt et al. 1996). Here reflectivity refers to an "internal process of attention and thought" (p. 3). This term, for me, also implies a process of internal dialogue in which varied configurations of self experience (e.g., affect states, thoughts, imagery, and so on) are creatively played with and tested out for the purpose of discovery and of making sense. One of the functions of the supervision relationship is to help facilitate this process. Neufeldt and colleagues (1966) address this from a more behavioral perspective: "Instead of immediately telling a supervisee what to do next, for instance, [the supervisor] can model a reflective stance and encourage trainees' own openness, active inquiry, and vulnerability" (p. 9). This process clearly involves a willingness to encourage exploration and a susceptibility toward meaningful interpersonal exchanges. This contrasts with the familiar syllogistic, lock-step approach to clinical "problem-solving." It invites creativity, novelty, reorganization, and of course, learning.

Searles (1955) focuses on the centrality of the reflection process in the supervision relationship and emphasizes that the supervisor's wide range of emotional experiences *vis-à-vis* the supervisee may often reflect countertransference reactions that help illuminate the patient–analyst relationship. Hora (1957) elaborates upon this phenomenon: "The supervisee unconsciously identifies with the patient and involuntarily behaves in such a manner as to elicit in the supervisor those very emotions which he himself experienced while working with the patient but was unable to convey verbally" (Grinberg 1970, p. 380). While useful regarding potential phenomena in the supervision relationship, this "parallelism" perspective tends to rely upon a one-person model in which the patient and her transference comprise the primary contributions to the dynamics at hand (Fosshage 1995). According to Fosshage, this perspective alone eliminates other vital, intersubjective dimensions to the supervision relationship, namely, the contributions of the supervisor and supervisee.

Mollon (1989) feels strongly about the capacity for reflection in the supervision setting and speaks about it as a state of mind "which is receptive and reflective, one which is open to impressions, perhaps somewhat akin to dreaming" (p. 120). He posits that the supervisor's task is correlated with Bion's (1977) description of how the "mother's reverie, her capacity to be emotionally receptive and thoughtful, which he terms 'alpha function,' may transform the raw elements of her infant's experience into material which has meaning, which can be thought about, dreamt about and communicated to others" (p. 120). He also states that the "supervisor's task is to help create a *space for thinking*, a space for reflection with a toleration for not knowing and not understanding . . . [u]ltimately the space for thinking must be internalized to form the capacity for internal supervision" (p. 120). One of the central aims of supervision is to foster this type of cognitive/affective experience in the supervisee.

An additional though particularly crucial consideration regarding the reflection process resides in the supervisee's experience immediately prior to embarking upon the supervision relationship; that is, it is instructive for the supervisee to reflect upon his cognitive/affective predisposition or subjectivity in approaching the supervisor and the supervision relationship in general. Unlike many patients at the outset of treatment, the supervisee, perhaps himself a patient, may be better situated and more inclined to reflect on this question. Due to previous experience and training, the supervisee may consider more readily questions such as "What transference propensities do I sense as I embark upon this new relationship?" Reflection in this domain can help clarify one's needs, expectations, and fears in relation to the supervision relationship; it can help clarify how one might organize external stimuli and consequently how one's subjectivity will contribute to the supervision experience. This in turn helps develop an understanding of the way in which the supervision experience will influence the nature of the patient's therapy.

What follows is a more specific view of the potential for reflection in this area. A male therapist initiates supervision with a highly experienced and accomplished clinician. The therapist asks himself, How do I feel about this person? How do I experience her? Do I trust her? Do I feel safe with her? How authentic and self-disclosing can I be with her? How comfortable do I feel with disagreeing with her? Is there an arbiter of truth here? If so, who is it? And if so, do I want there to be one? What is the outcome if, after extensive reflection, I continue to conflict with her perspective about my patient? What role do the exploration, examination, and discussion of countertransference play in this professional relationship? What is her perspective on countertransference, theoretically and practically? Where is the dividing line between supervision and treatment? The answers to these inquiries—and there are a multitude of additional questions to consider—will determine how this therapist ultimately will interact with his supervisor, and equally important, in what manner he will present and explore his case.

PRESENTING A CASE

The specific manner in which the therapist will present his case material is multi-determined; its origins are complex. First, consider the impact of the therapist's own transference propensities, his current treatment experience, the affective and interpersonal pressures placed upon him by his patient, the interpersonal impact of his supervisor, and in general his relative sense of safety in the professional setting. Then consider the impact of these variables upon the supervisor in conjunction with his (the supervisor's) own transference organization. Essentially, a complex network and interplay of transference–countertransference dynamics and resulting experiences will coalesce through the convergence of three (not two) unique psyches. This *convergence* has been addressed in different, captivating ways, but usually so in the context of the more traditional *parallelism phenomenon* alluded to above. Gediman and Wolkenfeld (1980) highlight the notion that

> [t]herapists manifest major psychic events in supervision, including complex behavior patterns, affects, and conflicts which parallel processes that are prominent in their interactions with their patients in the treatment situation. . . . A supervisor often discovers these parallelisms when certain of his emotional reactions lead him to realize that his supervisee is engaged unconsciously with him in a "tension system" which is similar to that occurring in the therapy situation. [pp. 234–236]

Additionally, Ekstein and Wallerstein (1958) note that what the therapist reports in supervision about his patient's sessions may often parallel difficulties he is experiencing in supervision with his supervisor.

Doehrman (1976) underscores the tendency of therapists to behave with their patients in concordance with or in opposition to their supervisor's behavior with them. She sees this as an enactment of or reaction against their supervisor's essential transference configurations. This is an aspect of the parallelism phenomenon, according to Gediman and Wolkenfeld (1980), and emphasizes even more the need for continual "recognition of the complex interactions among patient, analyst, and supervisor, which bond them in a systemic network . . ." (p. 241). In addition, Dombeck and Brody (1995) discuss the "principle of system parallel reflection [in which] the emotional process in the relationships of the client-family, the client-therapist, and the therapist-supervisor systems mirror each other" (p. 3). They state that "changes in the emotional process in each system is reflected in the other two" (p. 3).

It seems to me that, during the course of an intensive, ongoing supervision regarding one particular patient, the participants will benefit from reflecting upon how their subjective and constructed convictions about the patient have developed and continue to evolve. After all, I can imagine a multitude of ways in which to present a single patient to a supervisor, much of which is dependent upon many of the factors outlined above, including my affect coloration, my general health and energy level, my specific countertransference predisposition (in relation to my patient, as well as my supervisor), the presence of any still unrecognized unconscious communications from my patient, and so forth. In that regard, Gediman and Wolkenfeld (1980) note that "as supervising psychoanalysts we recognize that the therapist's report [of his or her patient] has been edited unconsciously and that through empathic identification the therapist has absorbed more than he can readily verbalize" (p. 251). One perspective about and presentation of the patient may not be any more "correct" or "accurate" than another, but one may potentially be more temporally salient and relevant than another. Reflecting upon how I "choose" (usually an unconscious decision) to present my case might reveal valuable and helpful information.

WILLINGNESS TO DISCLOSE

The potential value and utility of examining the foregoing supervision concerns hinge upon the relative willingness of both supervisor and supervisee to address these processes openly. This naturally could include a mutual, reciprocal, verbal exploration of both parties' countertransference experiences in relation to the patient at hand. What primarily differentiates this potentially treatment-like process from a treatment context is the continued and persistent focus upon the intended subject matter of supervision outlined above.[4] A facet of this exploration should extend to the supervisor's ongoing invitation to the supervisee to reflect upon how the supervision experience is impacting the supervisee from a cognitive, affective, theoretical, and/or practical standpoint. This facet, if left unattended, can alter the manner in which the supervisee presents his clinical material and potentially complicate, and perhaps obscure rather than illuminate, the vision of the elephant.

One area of informative research centers around the phenomenon of supervisee nondisclosure to the supervisor and the salience of what is not disclosed. Ladany and colleagues (1996) note that

> an implicit assumption in most psychotherapy supervision models is that for the supervisor to facilitate the development of therapeutic competence in the supervisee, the supervisee must disclose descriptive information about the client, the therapeutic interaction, *the supervisory interaction* [italics added], and personal information about himself or herself. . . . Nondisclosure would presumably interfere with the supervision process and thus inhibit trainee learning. . . . [I]t seems plausible to suspect that much of what is not disclosed in supervision may be as salient as, if not more salient than, what is disclosed. [p. 10]

---

4. Fosshage (1995) poignantly addresses the concern about supervision becoming treatment. He states, "the 'teach or treat' dichotomy is no longer a meaningful distinction, for 'treating' corresponds with illuminating the analyst's experience, a necessary process for 'teaching'" (p. 202).

The results of Ladany and colleagues' study reflect that 97.2 percent of supervisees do withhold information from their supervisors. The content of the nondisclosures centers around "negative reactions to the supervisor, personal issues not directly related to supervision, clinical mistakes, evaluation concerns, general client observations" (p. 17), as well as issues revolving around countertransference. Grinberg (1970) shares that a supervisee's anxiety can occasionally be intense enough that he will lie about the clinical material, which he "reconstructs to accord with his fantasy of what the supervisor prefers" (p. 377). It seems reasonable to consider that one significant source of supervisee nondisclosure revolves around an experienced lack of safety and potential for shame, devaluation, and perhaps political suicide.

Nondisclosure in this arena suggests the potential for there being at least two treatments with two patients, figuratively speaking: one that is conducted in the supervisee's office with his patient and another that is idiosyncratically constructed and discussed in the supervisor's office with his supervisor. As Fosshage recommends, providing the supervisee with a nonconfrontational, relatively safe environment in which he may illuminate his experience of self and other helps facilitate a better integration of the various facets of the elephant, or the "two treatments," into a more cohesive, intelligible whole.

In that vein, Ladany and colleagues rightly recommend that supervisors "inquire about supervisee reactions and strive toward relationships that have didactic, supportive, and collaborative components . . . if supervisors are going to improve the therapy provided by their supervisees, they may want to engage in an ongoing evaluative process of their work with their supervisees" (p. 22). This process has been referred to by Fleming and Benedek (1966) as the *learning alliance*. Gediman and Wolkenfeld (1980) define this concept as "the acceptance of a mutually shared educational goal involving expectations of giving and receiving help and initiating a bond of trust without which the work cannot proceed" (p. 249).

Nondisclosure on the part of the supervisor can be equally stifling and stagnating. Lederman (1982) contrasts the perspectives of Searles (1965) and Reich (1973) regarding the supervision experience. He notes that, from Searles' standpoint, the essence of the supervisor's armamentarium lies in "his experience and his emotions, particularly the emotions the supervisor experiences in the course of a supervisory relationship" (p. 424). Also, Black (1988) suggests that supervisor self-disclosure is an equally vital component in a successful supervision experience. Gitelson (1949), Ekstein and Wallerstein (1958), and Gediman and Wolkenfeld (1980) all observe the necessity of self-exposure to effect the learning process.

CLINICAL MATERIAL

The following vignette regarding a 30-year-old female patient with a history of depression illustrates how the subjective vision of a patient might unfold between supervisor and supervisee and how the delineation of the transference–countertransference configurations of all the parties contributes to this development. It also illuminates the importance of self-disclosure in the supervision setting.

Following some discussion about the supervisee's impressions of and countertransference to his patient, the supervisor inquired of the supervisee how he was experiencing this recent supervision process. This inquiry was initiated by the supervisor in response to her (the supervisor's) feeling rather tight, constricted, subdued, and inhibited during the hour. These feelings were accompanied by an impulse and image of being angry with the supervisee and shaking him by the shoulders. She wondered whether this reflected her own affective predisposition at that moment, whether it was a communication of an idiosyncratic aspect of the supervisee, or whether it was originally a part of the patient's affective experience and simply conveyed through the medium of the supervisee's cognitive/affective presentation (or, of course, a combination thereof).

The supervisee reflected upon his supervisor's question and responded that, while the recent supervision was helpful, he did not feel that she was actually getting a real sense of the patient at hand and that he consequently felt more alone in working with this patient than on previous occasions. He conveyed that the patient had been particularly challenging and difficult recently, and he felt that he needed substantial help right now. In effect, he felt that she was being somewhat subdued, almost withholding, in contrast to other occasions. The supervisor stated that she was feeling unusually constricted and that this was unfamiliar to her. She then inquired further as to how the supervisee thought these experiences might relate to the patient at hand. He responded that, on reflection, his personal experience of her, right now, was strikingly similar to how he had been experiencing his patient recently and that, in fact, this was the very quality he found so irritating and burdensome about the patient.

After further contact with the patient and continued reflection and discussion in supervision over the weeks to follow, it began to emerge that the patient's feelings of isolation and aloneness, of having to manage "all the burdens and terror on my own," coupled with the patient's experience of the therapist as sometimes withdrawn and constricted, frightened her into her own defensive withdrawal and constriction. This was ultimately conveyed and responded to in the context of supervision. The therapist further realized that he felt frightened, alone, and constricted as well in response to his own sense of helplessness with the patient. He speculated that his feelings originated from his patient's unconscious communications of her affect state and from his own transference configuration in relation to the patient. He later stated that among all of his fantasies about his patient, he often imagined shaking her and forcefully coercing her into assertiveness, openness, and independence. He had previously felt that these feelings and fantasies were of little importance, and they remained just on the periphery of his awareness until his countertransference exchanges with his supervisor. He later interpreted these experiences partly as a complementary identification (Racker 1968), engendered through the medium of an unconscious communication, and partly as his own transference-based response to a frustrating interpersonal exchange.

Ultimately, in the context of the countertransference interplay between her and her supervisee, the supervisor was able to experience the defensive, threatened component of both the patient and the therapist, as well as the complementary component of hostility and coercion. In addition, the supervisor was later able to disclose, after more reflection, that she herself felt somewhat withholding toward the supervisee—not unlike the way in which the supervisee had felt and sometimes behaved toward the patient. This, she concluded, was in response to her own experience of the supervisee as not behaving assertively enough and as indirectly communicating his feelings of dependency on the supervisor. The supervisor assimilated aspects of the supervisee's presentation in this manner, due in part to her own transference organization, and responded with resentment and ultimately withdrawal. This experience of withdrawal combined seamlessly with the patient's unconscious communication (via the supervisee) of a defensive affective withdrawal and search for greater safety.

DISCUSSION

The reflection, exploration, and discussion by supervisor and supervisee significantly augmented the sense and depth of the shared, subjective vision of the patient, as well as their shared experiences of their own subjectivities. This was largely based upon their susceptibility and willingness to engage in the countertransference and experiential portion of their relationship. This, in turn, facilitated a greater willingness on the part of the supervisee to examine ongoing countertransference experiences in relation to the patient and to take a broader, empathic step into the subjective world of the patient. In effect, each individual seemed willing in this instance to say, "Here—let me *show* you what I think this patient is like, what I am like when I have contact with this patient, and further, how my patient might experience me." This is an excellent example of what Windholz (1970) refers to in the supervision experience as the "unusual empathic processes which move from the student to the supervisor and back, leading to the anticipated changes in the patient" (p. 394).

In addition to the clinical, utilitarian value inherent in these exchanges, the supervisee was able to reap the benefits of a "new object experience" (Shane and Shane 1989) in a professional setting. He experienced his supervisor as an affectively curious and reflective professional being, who was willing empathically to immerse herself in the process—that is, admit some degree of her embeddedness in the relationship—and to demonstrate working with countertransference in a practical manner. This was a powerful source of identification and internalization, for the supervisee, of supervisor containing, reflecting, and relating functions. This generally aided his continued development of his capacity to enjoy a wider range of cognitive/affective experiences in a professional setting. Stolorow (1993) observes that "if an interpretation is to produce a therapeutic effect, it must provide the patient with a *new experience of being deeply understood*" (p. 47, italics original). This is similar to what ideally the supervisor conveys to the supervisee, if the supervisory "interpretations" (based on the supervisor's affective attunements and cognitive intuition regarding the supervisee and his patient) are to produce an identifiable and enduring set of developmental experiences.

CONCLUSION

Clinical research and experience point to the need for close examination and exploration of transference–countertransference configurations in the supervision relationship. The continuous unfolding and illumination of the experiences of all three participants and the clarification of the supervisee's direction with his patient center around the willingness of supervisee and supervisor alike to address these processes and events verbally. Additionally, this willingness fosters the potential for a developmental experience that may greatly contribute to the supervisee's continued self-awareness and personal growth.

REFERENCES

Bion, W. R. (1977). *Seven Servants.* New York: Jason Aronson.

Black, B. (1988). Components of effective and ineffective psychotherapy supervision as perceived by supervisees with different levels of clinical experience. (Doctoral dissertation, Columbia University, 1987). *Dissertation Abstracts International* 48, 3105B.

Doehrman, M. J. G. (1976). Parallel processes in supervision and psychotherapy. *Bulletin of the Menninger Clinic* 40:3–104.

Dombeck, M. T., and Brody, S. L. (1995). Clinical supervision: a three-way mirror. *Archives of Psychiatric Nursing* 9(1): 3–10.

Ekstein, R., and Wallerstein, R. S. (1958). *The Teaching and Learning of Psychotherapy.* New York: Basic Books.

Fleming, J., and Benedek, T. F. (1966). *Psychoanalytic Supervision: A Method of Clinical Teaching.* New York: Grune & Stratton.

Fosshage, J. (1995). Toward a model of psychoanalytic supervision from a self psychological/intersubjective perspective. In *Psychodynamic Supervision: Issues for the Supervisor and Supervisee,* ed. M. Rock, pp. 189–210. Northvale, NJ: Jason Aronson.

Gediman, H. K., and Wolkenfeld, F. (1980). The parallelism phenomenon in psychoanalysis and supervision: its reconstruction as a triadic system. *Psychoanalytic Quarterly* 49:234–255.

Gitelson, M. (1949). *Concerning the problem of countertransference.* Discussion of papers by T. F. Benedek and E. Weiss at Chicago Psychoanalytic Society.

Grinberg, L. (1970). The problems of supervision in psychoanalytic education. *International Journal of Psycho-Analysis* 51(3):371–383.

Hora, T. (1957). Contribution to the phenomenology of the supervisory process. *American Journal of Psychotherapy* 11:769–773.

Kovacs, V. (1936). Training and control analysis. *International Journal of Psycho-Analysis* 17:346–354.

Ladany, N., Hill, C. E., Corbett, M. M., and Nutt, E. A. (1996). Nature, extent, and importance of what psychotherapy trainees do not disclose to their supervisors. *Journal of Counseling Psychology* 43(1):10–24.

Lederman, S. (1982). A contribution to the theory and practice of supervision. *Psychoanalytic Review* 69(4):423–439.

Lewin, B. D., and Ross, H. (1960). *Psychoanalytic Education in the United States.* New York: Norton.

Lichtenberg, J. D. (1991). The theory of motivational-functional systems as psychic structures. In *The Concept of Structure in Psychoanalysis*, ed. T. Shapiro, pp. 57–72. Madison, CT: International Universities Press.

Mollon, P. (1989). Anxiety, supervision and a space for thinking: some narcissistic perils for clinical psychologists in learning psychotherapy. *British Journal of Medical Psychology* 62(2):113–122.

Neufeldt, S. A., Karno, M. P., and Nelson, M. L. (1996). A qualitative study of experts' conceptualization of supervisee reflectivity. *Journal of Counseling Psychology* 43(1):3–9.

Racker, H. (1968). *Transference and Countertransference.* New York: International Universities Press.

Reich, A. (1973). *Psychoanalytic Contributions.* New York: International Universities Press.

Ricci, W. (1995). Self and intersubjectivity in the supervision process. *Bulletin of the Menninger Clinic* 59(1):53–68.

Searles, H. F. (1955). The informational value of the supervisor's emotional experiences. *Psychiatry* 18:135–146.

———. (1965). *Collected Papers on Schizophrenia and Related Subjects.* New York: International Universities Press.

Shane, E., and Shane, M. (1989). Developmental perspectives in psychoanalysis: prologue. *Psychoanalytic Inquiry* 9(3):333–339.

Stolorow, R. (1993). The nature and therapeutic action of psycho-
    analytic interpretation. In *The Intersubjective Perspective*, ed.
    R. Stolorow, G. Atwood, and B. Brandchaft, pp. 43–55. North-
    vale, NJ: Jason Aronson.
———. (1995). An intersubjective view of self psychology. *Psycho-
    analytic Dialogues* 5(3):393–399.
Stolorow, R., Brandchaft, B., and Atwood, G. (1987). *Psychoana-
    lytic Treatment: An Intersubjective Approach*. Hillsdale, NJ: Ana-
    lytic Press.
Windholz, E. (1970). The theory of supervision in psychoanalytic
    education. *International Journal of Psycho-Analysis* 51(3):393–
    406.

Credits

The editor gratefully acknowledges permission to reprint material from the following sources.

Chapter 1, "The Changing Scene in Psychoanalytic Supervision," here titled "The Changing Scene in Supervision," by Stanley H. Teitelbaum, from *Psychoanalysis and Psychotherapy* 12(2):183–192. Copyright © 1995 by International Universities Press and used by permission of the publisher and the author.

Chapter 2, "Narcissistic Vulnerability in Psychoanalytic Psychotherapy Supervisees: Ego Ideals, Self-Exposure and Narcissistic Character Defenses," here titled "Narcissistic Vulnerability in Supervisces: Ego Ideals, Self-Exposure, and Narcissistic Character Defenses," by Susan Gill, from *International Forum of Psychoanalysis* 8:1–6. Copyright © 1999 by Scandinavian University Press, and used by permission of the publisher and the author.

tion for the Advancement of Psychotherapy and used by permission of the publisher and the author.

Chapter 13, "When Supervisor and Therapist Dream: The Use of an Unusual Countertransference Phenomenon," by Anne E. Bernstein and Susan C. Katz, from *Journal of the American Academy of Psychoanalysis* 15(2):261–271. Copyright © 1987 by the American Academy of Psychoanalysis and used by permission of the publisher and the authors.

Chapter 14, "The Vision in Supervision: Transference–Countertransference Dynamics and Disclosure in the Supervision Relationship," here titled "Transference–Countertransference Dynamics and Disclosure in Supervision," by William J. Coburn, from *Bulletin of the Menninger Clinic* 61:481–494. Copyright © 1997 by The Guilford Press and used by permission of the publisher and the author.

Index

242   INDEX